PRAISE FOR FIERCE, FREE, AND FULL OF FIRE

"Here's the truth: Jen has been pushing me out of my comfort zone like a loving big sister for over a decade, and that's exactly what reading this book is like, in the best possible way: like sitting across from someone who loves you enough to tell you the truth and light up your heart and set you free. I want every woman in my life to read this book—every single one."

—Shauna Niequist, *New York Times* bestselling author of *Present Over Perfect*

"Some books are all in the head or all in the heart, others are all in the hustle or the habit, but this book is blood and bone and soul. It pulses with energy and heat, with sincerity and goodness, strength and truth. It is beautifully written, sincerely good, authentically lived absolutely, but I also believe it will literally save lives. I cannot wait to press this book into the hands of every woman I know. Jen has never settled for the wide and easy path. She chases after Jesus and redraws the margins as the center of God's kin-dom but like any true disciple of Jesus, she always leaves a path for us to follow too. A good guide who is worthy of your trust, Jen has offered us more than a map or a guidebook, this is truly a path for transformation, wholeness, and freedom for the sake of the world. I love this book and I love her."

—Sarah Bessey, author of *Jesus Feminist* and *Miracles and Other Reasonable Things*

"You will be delighted by Jen's stories of pre-adolescence. You will resonate with her moments of self-doubt. You will drink deeply from her words of affirmation. But in this book, the greatest gift Jen offers us is the language to navigate a world that is unkind to women, but desperately needs us. This is not the 'women's Christian living' book of old. If we let them, Jen's words just might release our fierceness, give us the push we need to choose freedom, and in so doing set the world on fire."

—Austin Channing Brown, author of *I'm Still Here: Black Dignity in a World Made for Whiteness*

"Spending time with Jen Hatmaker, in person or on the page, invariably reminds me just how much possibility there is in this life. She is tuned for connection and offers up a pretty damn fearless point of view here, something we could all use a hearty dose of."

—Kelly Corrigan, *New York Times* bestselling author
of *The Middle Place* and *Tell Me More*

"Our spiritual journeys are as personal, nuanced, and diverse as we women are, but they are also beautifully interdependent. More than ever, we need to cheer each other on, even and especially in spite of our differences. Jen leads this charge inviting us into her hard-won and often hilarious spiritual lessons learned, and in so doing, inspires us in our own good/hard work of uncovering who we are as women, who God is, and what we are to do with it."

—Katherine Wolf, survivor, advocate, and author
of *Suffer Strong* and *Hope Heals*

"I often read books and find myself ferociously taking notes for myself to reference later—but in *Fierce, Free, and Full of Fire*, I find myself taking notes for me, my friends, and my daughters. The message that we have to grant ourselves grace, while holding ourselves to a standard of excellence (not perfection!), is timeless and legacy worthy. This is a must-read book for today—and for generations to come."

—Nicole Walters, CEO, Inherit Learning Company; TV personality,
and Mama of three girls, www.NicoleWalters.com

"What Jen gives us in this book is not solely inspiration, but the tools we need to help us live the life that is meant for us as individuals. There is no shame here, no 'shoulding.' There is no hype or hustle culture. Not here, not in this book. Rather, there are illuminated paths for us to walk toward a life that feels more fully our own. You will finish this book feeling seen, respected, and ready to do the work not of changing yourself but uncovering yourself. This book is the work of a woman doing the work, an invitation to all of us to join in. We do not need to be reinvented, just rediscovered. Thank you, Jen, for walking alongside us."

—Nora McInerny, author of *No Happy Endings*; host
of *Terrible, Thanks for Asking* podcast

"Only Jen can have you laughing during the second sentence of an introduction, standing to fist bump the air by the middle, and then crying in a heap by book's end. Jen embraces the paradoxical tensions most of us want to ignore while encouraging us to hold space for the unfamiliar, scary, or seemingly unsafe things of this world. No matter where you are on life's journey, you will find yourself in these pages."

—Jessica Honneger, founder and co-CEO of Noonday
Collection; author of *Imperfect Courage*

FIERCE *Free* AND FULL OF FIRE

The Guide to Being Glorious You

JEN HATMAKER

NELSON BOOKS

An Imprint of Thomas Nelson

Published in Nashville, Tennessee, by Nelson Books, an imprint of Thomas Nelson. Nelson Books and Thomas Nelson are registered trademarks of HarperCollins Christian Publishing, Inc.

Published in association with Yates & Yates, www.yates2.com.

Thomas Nelson titles may be purchased in bulk for educational, business, fund-raising, or sales promotional use. For information, please e-mail SpecialMarkets@ThomasNelson.com.

Scripture quotations marked THE MESSAGE are from *The Message*. Copyright © by Eugene H. Peterson 1993, 1994, 1995, 1996, 2000, 2001, 2002. Used by permission of NavPress. All rights reserved. Represented by Tyndale House Publishers, Inc.

Scripture quotations marked NLT are from the Holy Bible, New Living Translation. © 1996, 2004, 2007, 2013, 2015 by Tyndale House Foundation. Used by permission of Tyndale House Publishers, Inc., Carol Stream, Illinois 60188. All rights reserved.

Any Internet addresses, phone numbers, or company or product information printed in this book are offered as a resource and are not intended in any way to be or to imply an endorsement by Thomas Nelson, nor does Thomas Nelson vouch for the existence, content, or services of these sites, phone numbers, companies, or products beyond the life of this book.

ISBN 978-1-4002-2241-4 (signed)
ISBN 978-0-7180-8816-3 (eBook)
ISBN 978-0-7180-8814-9 (HC)

Library of Congress Control Number: 2020931914

Printed in the United States of America
20 21 22 23 24 LSC 10 9 8 7 6 5 4 3 2 1

For the women in my family, some of the greatest loves of my life: my mom, Jana, and my sisters, Lindsay and Cortney; my mother-in-law, Jacki; my sisters-in-law, Lana and Sarah; and my nieces, Rachel and Rebekah. My beloved daughters, Sydney and Remy. What great luck to belong to this family of strong women. You are my North Star. This book is for you and because of you. May fierceness, freedom, and fire reign in our family for generations.

CONTENTS

HOW I CONNECT

INTRODUCTION

I grew up around well-behaved women. They were mostly suburban church moms who didn't drink, never cussed, and sang in the Christmas cantatas. Do not get me wrong for one second: I loved them, my mom's and grandma's friends, the consortium of bonus moms who helped raise me. But, seriously, they behaved. My mom drank a single glass of wine at Disney World once when I was in sixth grade, and I remember thinking this must be what it felt like just before your parent became an alcoholic.

I had no other standard bearers to follow. I barely saw women in civic leadership, corporate management, and certainly not the pulpit. The women in my life were all smart and capable, but they rode in the passenger seat. My world was comfortably maintained by Men in Charge and, although they were good to their wives and daughters and certainly reliant on their endless behind-the-scenes labor, the lady stencil was pretty homogenous. Thus I nestled my identity somewhere inside the confines of those norms. I was set up to succeed there as a Type A rule-follower, thirsty for affirmation and irrationally defensive of the status quo. I never met a rule I didn't like, and I was prepared to grow up and behave better than any girl had ever behaved, which was my version of ambition.

Ironically, it was women who chipped away at my template.

Isn't it always the women?

First there was Mrs. Prissy, aptly named and worthy of her moniker. Where my mom and the rest were practical and modest, Mrs. Prissy dressed head to toe in leopard print and let us know in no uncertain terms she planned to become well-acquainted with plastic surgery. No, she was not going to go gently into that good night. She kept her outrageous jewelry in a double-decker tackle box and gave us all nicknames we use to this living day. Mrs. Prissy was super-model gorgeous and obscenely stylish. She blew my mind. My sisters and I couldn't get enough of her. She was wild when everyone else was proper, and she took up more space than I thought women were allotted. I assumed she was just a one-off, but her specific sense of self with no apologies challenged my tidy categories.

Later, it was the Lady Deacons at our first church out of college. Unbeknownst to us, my husband, Brandon, and I had accidentally joined forces with the liberal Baptists (which our conservative Oklahoma compatriots let us know right quick). They were as exotic to me as snake handlers. I was scared to tell my parents, lest they assume we had, as my friend Alex's father said when he slid over from Catholicism, "lost the faith." The Lady Deacons didn't just pass the offering plates. They were in leadership and the pulpit and at all the meetings; they helped steer the ship. There are no words to describe this revelation. I literally had no idea this was possible. I remember watching a woman preach, practical and modest in the way I understood but also carefully dissecting a complicated bit of Scripture. I looked around like, *Oh, my word! These folks are taking her seriously and no one is going up in flames, and I am so happy my parents aren't visiting this weekend.* Her spiritual authority rubbed against two decades of internalized patriarchy, and I couldn't decide if she was my enemy or my hero.

A while later, as I was coming into some sense of my own mind and my internal wiring was threatening to become a problem in both personality and function, it was Anne Lamott who shocked me anew. A close friend, more aware than I was of my own shifting North Star, put her book *Traveling Mercies* in my hands, and the lights flickered on, then blazed to life. Not once, not even close to once, had I ever heard a woman . . . author . . . Christian . . . talk like that. And it wasn't just her saucy conversion story where she compared Jesus to a stray cat who wouldn't leave her alone until she finally cursed and said, "I quit. All right. You can come in," but she offered such naked truth telling, so little self-protection, zero rules followed. Anne existed in a world I'd never even heard of. I had no access to a community that allowed this type of faith. I didn't know a woman could write like that, think like that, much less succeed like that. I had no idea who was giving her this permission. Why wasn't she getting in trouble?

More recently, it was the women of the world who shifted my perspective, specifically the women of Ethiopia—more to the point, my adopted son Ben's mom. Sentayu is a marvel. After Ben and Remy were with us a couple of years, Brandon went back to Ethiopia to work with our partners there, and I told him, "We have to find Ben's mom." Pause. "And by *we* I mean *you*. It's just one woman in a country. Go with God." And he did. And we discovered a story full of abuse and betrayal and pain and loss, as all adoption stories begin with sorrow. But this smart, resourceful survivor, who once lived at the mercy of dishonorable men, went on to graduate from a yearlong women's empowerment program, started her own coffee and tea shop, hired two girls off the streets as her first employees, remarried a good, good man, had two more beautiful sons, and bought a house.

As we sat in Sentayu's shop and home last year, Ben tucked into the crook of her arm, I thought, *Women are the baddest of badasses, and there is nothing they cannot overcome and accomplish.* She did this. With every odd against her, she chased down a dream and rebuilt her entire life out of grit, and now she is a business owner, homeowner, and proud wife and mom. I want to hoist her on my shoulders and carry her around the public square.

Women have continued to stretch and challenge me, teach and change me. Their voices from the margins have been particularly thought provoking, offering perspectives I've never before considered. Their experiences have given shape to my own inner tensions and language to my big questions. My worldview has expanded, and I've blown straight through whatever tidy category I once assumed I'd occupy, to both the great delight and despair of a watching world. But here is the magical place I landed:

I finally clearly know who I am and how I was made, how I thrive and what I'm here for, what I believe and what I care about, and I'm not afraid to walk in that, even when it doesn't fit the mold. I am finally the exact same on the outside as I actually am on the inside without posturing, posing, or pretending.

Once I learned to understand and boldly claim the real me, my inside voice became my outside voice. Polished Me died, and Real Me came to life. I took ownership of my personality, ideas, convictions, and gifts, costs counted and paid. I looked complicated tension in the eye and refused to make excuses for staying sidelined. I chose to be okay when I took a remarkably different path than some of my peers, although that road was and still is sometimes lonely. I'd reached a dead end on what I could do while masquerading—professionally, relationally, spiritually. There was nowhere else to go except to slowly die inside. I decided that people-pleasing, fear, and politeness weren't the hallmarks of a well-lived life, nor were their ugly companions: passive aggression, resentment, and dishonesty. I discovered the world is hungry for women who show up and tell the truth, unafraid and free, expanding to the very edges of who they were always meant to be.

It is *that* woman who brings her gifts to bear on this earth. The one who refuses to shrink on demand, who takes ownership of her precious wiring and encourages her sisters to do likewise. That woman refuses to contort to a template but rather occupies her own life as the recipient of God's unending favor, not a beggar at his door. This kind of woman also wants this freedom for everyone else; I cannot overstate this important correlation and how necessary it is right now. She craves a genuine world, a more honest and sincere community, relationships based in truth telling, to be refreshing to a parched world. She is not afraid of herself, so she is unafraid of others.

She is fierce.

She is free.

She is full of fire.

This brings me to you, dear one. If you are new to me, then welcome. My space will be safe for you, and you are loved already. But if you've been with me for some time, you know I've done this work. You know it cost me. You also know it brought me to life, and I feel like I am breathing clean air for the first time. I'm not afraid anymore. In these pages I will offer you absolutely everything I learned, because I want this for you too.

Hiding and posing and pretending is exhausting. Full stop. Doesn't it sound like a relief to have it all match? The inside and the outside, the real life and the displayed life? Spoiler alert: this is possible, and you and everyone you love will flourish when it happens. Sorry to give away the last page, but even that very private, terrifying thing you are thinking of, that secret, that question you are asking, that dream, that need, that buried anger, that delicious desire, it can all live in the open, and its unveiling be your liberation song. Come get your life!

Together, let's unweave the beautiful threads that make each of us exactly who we are and have a good look at them. Let's name them and own them, celebrate them and claim them. Rather than excuse, hide, or aw-shucks the stuff that makes us human, the ways in which we thrive, we will honor them by exploring the following five areas: who I am, what I need, what I want, what I believe, and how I connect. These are the categories that make up a whole life. I cannot trace a single element of substance that doesn't uplink to one of these chambers. How you are wired, what you actually need, the stash of dreams you harbor, your deepest convictions, and the health of your relationships are your entire world. Those are the containers in which everything else of your lived experience exists, and they inform every word you say, decision you make, work you engage, and manner in which you love. These are the building blocks of the life you are constructing, and you must lay them with care.

Some of these chapters will hit you right in the feels, and others might not. My hypothesis is that every reader will need some of these in a crucial way, some in a medium way, and some not at all. You may be in solid possession of *what I need* but absolutely bankrupt on *what I want*. Maybe *who I am* is not a mystery but *what I believe* is a fuzzy, hot mess. As your devoted author, I absolutely noticed the chapters where I was still slogging away or freshly tender compared to others where I was more like, NOW HEAR THIS, WORLD. My point is to take what you need here. If you discover that you are beautifully healthy in several areas, pop some champagne and don't feel pressured to invent tension where there is none. Rather, press in to the chapters where you have more to learn, more to explore, more to disclose, more to develop. You'll have a few. I literally *wrote the book* and still have a few.

You are a spectacular gift to this world, and we need you. You have work to do, and you have to show up real to do it. The crafted version of you cannot pull it off. The silenced and sidelined version of you will never be up to the task. Buried talents are a bona fide tragedy, as Jesus liked to say. Your place and space are irreplaceable; they are so incredibly yours alone to occupy. It's so exciting. Your precious life! Your good and beautiful soul. Your giftedness and dreams. Your steady convictions and faithfulness. The family and neighbors who love you so. This is your one life, and you get to live it absolutely truthfully.

One last note before we dive in: there is no one way to be nor some Jen-emulating agenda I'm advocating for. My path toward wholeness landed me here, but your endgame will look entirely different, as well it should. I am not interested in building a community of Jenions, so don't waste one second worrying that I am lighting a path that makes absolutely zero sense for you, your personality, your community, or your trajectory. You will get to the end of this work and discover *your* feet planted firmly in *your* life, thank goodness, because that is where you live. That is where your people are. That is the community you serve. That is where your impossibly dear self is needed. The work is similar, but the results will look different. And we'll end up having healthy, liberated women planted in every corner, like seeds of outrageous flourishing, bringing things back to life.

Isn't it always the women?

WHO I AM

1

I AM WIRED THIS WAY

My sixth-grade teacher, Mrs. Anderson, hated me. Freshly emerged from my timid, nerdy shell, I was finally ready to party. I faced the world like a sunflower to the sun and started slicing through the dicey melee of middle school. I had ideas. I had thoughts. I had an abundance of words. I discovered I was funny, which was decent currency since my haircut suggested "1985 softball coach" and my plastic glasses were identical to my Aunt Wilda's. Awakened to the social vacuum that *clearly craved a leader,* I nominated myself and took office.

Mrs. Anderson was here for exactly none of it. She favored the boys and didn't like me or my mouth. In a moment she came to regret once my dad caught wind of it, she pulled my friends aside and asked, "Why are you even friends with her? She is so domineering," which they tattled to me about immediately because you can't trust a sixth-grade girl posse as far as you can stretch their phone cords. (In her defense now, I would be at severe risk of committing mass homicide if I had to manage a classroom of twelve-year-olds. Jesus would have to take every wheel. It is a wonder she showed up for work every day.)

But I was just a weird kid feeling her way through pre-adolescence. I was never mean or bad; I was just a lot. I felt her disapproval. I saw it in her body language, her facial expressions, her tone of voice. Even after she was forced to apologize for stirring the already churning pot of sixth-grade drama, she engaged me through clenched teeth. I tried mightily to right the ship with academic perfection and good behavior, my tricks of the trade, but straight A's weren't Mrs. Anderson's love language and I couldn't crack the code. I was already wobbly in my own skin, confused by my body and brain and feelings and fears, but her message came through and I received it:

She doesn't like who I am.

It packed such a wallop that I am still talking about it thirty-two years later.

As we lean in together for these next two hundred pages or so, there is much to discuss on what we do, what we are dreaming up, how our beliefs shape our lives, and how we navigate relationships, but I would love to start here with you: who you are. Just plain, without all the stuff attached to it yet. Way at the core of you—your personality, your wiring, the way you naturally live on this earth. Sometimes we're afraid or ashamed of it or don't quite know exactly what it is—the real us—because we've tamped it down for so long in response to others' approval or disapproval. But if we concede this ownership, we can forget everything else. Understanding and embracing who we are, how we've been created, is the launching pad for living a fearlessly genuine life, where we're no longer pretending or trying to be something other than what we are on the inside.

This seems obvious and easy, so why is it so hard? Why do

women get hung up here? Why is this one of the first areas where we start pretending?

Probably because we can adjust "how we act" or "what we say" to fit any context (women have a lifetime of practice), but "who we are" is the raw material of our perceived worth. If our core personality is up for critique, we've truly lost our central anchor. The human craving to be loved for *who we are* outside of *what we do* is so primal. It is densely bound with ideas of worth, value, and belonging. We assign great meaning to how much we are accepted, which is, of course, a function of how truly we are actually known. It is why Mrs. Anderson's disapproval of my very personality outside of performance was so rattling; it signaled that I was unlovable.

So we start there, because no one is unlovable. We were literally created by love, with love, and for love by a God who loves us and is Love itself. Its extravagance is almost embarrassing. And this love is not just for one type of person the world finds most acceptable; it's for all of us. If this isn't true, then nothing is true.

I find the diversity in our inner wiring fascinating; it feels creative and ballsy and wild. I like it. I can get behind a Creator who is uninhibited by homogeny. There is no typecast in humanity, no categories for Okay, Good, Better, and Best—at least not theoretically. In practice, unfortunately, we absolutely do assign value for Okay, Good, Better, and Best. Although those categories shift to fit the norms of any given group culture, we get the message early on that certain personalities are favored and others are a burden. This is not a mystery. Most women can read the room and understand what is expected, what will be rewarded with belonging and advantages. Our rules and alliances and power structures have clear bias toward (and against) particular "types."

Let me pick one of my worlds as an example: I used to be a darling in the subculture of evangelical women. I was literally groomed to succeed there. The preferred personality of a female leader in that context is funny and self-deprecating, bright and shiny, deferential and familiar. Let me clarify with backlighting: that community gravitates to star power, but primarily within its cultural norms. When those are challenged, the mechanism unravels, which means your personality should appropriately dazzle but not dissent.

To be fair, let me assess another world I am frequently associated with: the progressive activist community. My faith compels me into activism, so there is no alternative path for me. But when I first stepped toward that community, I received a different set of personality expectations, a new standard for admission into that leadership cabal: aggressive and forceful, mostly inflexible, confident in your expertise without muddying the waters with nuance. I am expected to weigh in on every fight, every issue, every daily land mine. My faith is sometimes a clunky companion in this world where I see it as central, because organized religion is incredibly suspect outside the steeples. In an odd parallel to the aversion to dissent I experienced in the subculture of evangelical women, the progressive community also participates in today's Cancel Culture for mistakes or diverging ideas—*you better step correct or GIRL, BYE.*

Threading this needle is the weirdest work of my life. And you can see the dilemma: if I craft my personality around pleasing the intended audience, the target never quits moving and, in chasing it, I forfeit who I actually am. I've tried this and—please listen to me—it is exhausting and confusing and doesn't work. The different versions of you end up competing and contradicting. You know it, and eventually others know it. The only relief is being genuine at all times with all people, and if you think that is also hard, you are correct, ma'am. But at least it is honest. At least it is whole and true. At least you don't have to adjust the station according to the passengers.

In *Braving the Wilderness*, Brené Brown calls this embracing of who you really are *true belonging*:

> True belonging is the spiritual practice of believing in and belonging to yourself so deeply that you can share your most authentic self with the world and find sacredness in both being a part of something and standing alone in the wilderness. True belonging doesn't require you to change who you are; it requires you to be who you are . . . True belonging is not something that you negotiate externally, it's what you carry in your heart. It's finding the sacredness in being a part of something and in braving the wilderness alone.[1]

Brené is not wrong about that wilderness, the place where you stand outside expectations no matter the cost (and there is one and we'll get to that). But I'd love to hover over this idea of internal belonging, this sense of self-awareness that provides an anchor no matter the waves or wind. I suspect we are all over the spectrum here, from the most self-assured to those with absolutely no idea who they are, or why. Additionally, our various environments have different expectations that affect our capacity to engage this identification. Some communities are more charitable and less afraid of diversity. Others highly value unanimity and thus build in consequences for defectors. So this work is harder for some of us by virtue of our setting.

My internal wiring is a conundrum for folks, as I mentioned earlier, and for ages, it was for me. I could not make sense of myself. This may sound off brand, but I actually like simple categories even as I encourage us to reject them. Labels and sound bites have always given me a handle on chaos. If I can reduce a thing down to a clearly defined core, it helps me make sense of all its tentacles. This has its place, as I am good at condensing complicated data to manageable chunks, but it has interfered with self-identification. When "rogue" elements of my makeup started popping up like whack-a-mole, I saw them as defects and doubled down on my "fixed" qualities.

For instance, returning to my previous example, at one point I positively thought I would flourish as a female leader in evangelical subculture for the rest of my life, as I embodied so many of its valued traits (and still do). I waxed and polished those elements of my circuitry and put them into high rotation. They worked! I got all the gold stars! I built a whole career, a sanctioned ministry.

Any discerning observer plainly noticed the places that were rubbing repeatedly, ultimately leading to a tear in the fabric. I, however, kept trying to patch up the alliance with good behavior. After a serious online challenge against, say, excluding women from church leadership or a robust defense of Black Lives Matter, once I had been #unfollowed, I'd intentionally present nothing but agreeable concepts, unimpeachable scriptures, and entertaining content for weeks. I *had* to find a way to keep my pesky prophetic nature from coming in like a wrecking ball. If I could just "not be political" like people insisted and divorce justice issues from my faith, I could salvage this. Other leaders were doing it. Why couldn't I?

Answer: because I actually couldn't. I am entirely wired to see, lament, and confront injustice. This is not a thing I do. This is who I am. My parents confirm this from the preschool years, that *full of fire* part of me. I will never thrive in any environment where I must stay silent in order to belong. That is the death knell. Let the bells toll.

Quid pro quo: taking that hard-won lesson into the activist community meant that when my faith was belittled or mischaracterized, when I felt the same instinct to curate faith content out to fit in better, I just carried it right into the middle of the room instead. Same reason: I actually couldn't leave it behind. I am entirely wired to love and believe in Jesus. This is not a thing I do. This is who I am. I believe God created me with a high capacity for things of the spirit, and there is no credible way for me to be anything else.

The deepest parts of who we are rise up. They can't help it.

Let's pay attention to them and give them a proper home in our lives, whether they fit tidily into all the categories or not.

Here I wave a red flag potentially for you. You might understand yourself based on faulty data, and it is worth sussing out. Scads of grown women assess their core identity based on what someone told them as kids, or through the lens of trauma, or from the perspective of their parents, or based on an old label. This is common. One of my closest friends, Laura, excels at friendship. She friends so hard; she is one of the most loyal, attentive, emotionally connected people I know. And yet she said once, "I never had any girlfriends growing up, because I am so bad at friendship." The rest of us gaped at her: "Who told you that?" It didn't occur to her that someone could be very wrong about her, so she never thought to question it.

If your mom always commented on how bossy you were, you might be locked into that notion. If someone harmed or abused you, that may have unfairly shaped your identity. You could have just grown without shedding the outdated container. Or you may have spent a decade squeezing yourself into the preferred mold for your career or role or community simply because you wanted to fit; belonging is a powerful incentive. My point is to be aware of the potential for bad intel. The compulsion to default to an imprecise stereotype of your own self is strong.

If I've done the work well, and I think I have, I understand myself now to be an interesting mix of competing qualities: I am assertive with a deep moral compass toward justice. I am also funny, silly, sarcastic, hyperbolic; I cherish humor. Funny is so fun, and I love it. Inside those twin pillars, I am tender but don't love showing it, ambitious but conflicted on how that manifests, and authentic but with an instinct to pretend if it shields me. In summation: assertive but funny, tender but wary, ambitious but reluctant, and fully transparent except when I'm not.

Please direct me to the section in the bookstore where this author fits.

It took me a long time to shake this down. There is no clearly defined subgroup that values all these qualities. If you meet me through one portal, say, humor writing, my serious advocacy side will jack you into left field when it shows up. If you found me through parenting leadership, some of it very tender, you will be shook when I announce on Instagram on a particularly bad day that "I love Jesus but hate at least half the people he created." *I said I was sorry.* Listen, I have TRIED to be the one thing for the one group, but I just cannot. I end up lying too much or eating my feelings or simmering in resentment, and I'm not a mental health expert, but that feels potentially ruinous.

This is why this work of understanding your identity comes first. It's why "who I am" matters. Having a handle on how you were created to function and flourish is your guide and, ultimately, your mooring. This informs all the other outcroppings we will discuss and makes sense of what you need and want, how you believe and act, how you love and connect. Dallas Willard said it like this:

> What is running your life at any given moment is your soul. Not external circumstances, not your thoughts, not your intentions, not even your feelings, but your soul. The soul is that aspect of your whole being that correlates, integrates, and enlivens everything going on in the various dimensions of the self. The soul is the life center of human beings.[2]

A brief word on my perspective: while not all my readers are faith folk—and, obviously, they are as welcomed and cherished as any—you probably know that I am a hippie-dippy, Big Love Jesus Type. So, up front, I sincerely believe God loves you and me like a crazed, obsessed parent who will never shut up about us. I believe we are precious and wanted and crafted and purposed, every one of us. God knows you and knows me, because he had a real hand in thinking us up. And he "created our inmost being," exactly the thing we are drilling into here. Your inmost being is a masterpiece of divine creativity, and whatever you discover in mining the depths of your soul, it is a great and glorious good for the world and was always meant to be. You are loved and lovable; this is my spiritual thesis. Your inmost being is worth uncovering.

In my experience, this exploratory work is made up of a combination of enough lived years, observable patterns, intentional investigation, and feedback from our closest people.

Let me pick through each of these components, starting with enough lived years. This is admittedly a wobbly metric, which I hold up more by touch than by book. Our understanding of who we are comes into focus the longer we reside in adulthood. Early on, it is still tangled up in childhood and adolescence, norms and expectations—unchallenged by real life. As someone not naturally self-aware, it took plenty of lived adult years for me to finally notice that who I was inside was not entirely the same as the me I projected. This is the exact meaning of disintegration—to separate into parts, to lose intactness. When this environment gets one part of you but that environment gets another, when you tuck away one piece in front of this crew but pull it out proudly for that one, when the hidden you is screaming in protest because she is not allowed to speak, whatever felt solid about your core self-dismantles. This is an unhappy, unhealthy way to live.

Again, this seems to become clearer the longer we live. Show me a grandma who has zero effs to give anymore, wearing what she wants, saying what she says, worrying exactly no seconds about anyone's opinions, and I will pledge my allegiance to her flag and offer to carry her tapestry bag wherever her journey doth take her. Reader, this internal clarity may be easier or harder to locate depending on how many days on earth you've logged. In my twenties, I would have been in an adjacent zip code. In my thirties, I moved into the neighborhood, and here in the middle of my forties, I'm home.

That said, if you have moved through a couple of decades, you may notice that some of your interior patterns have changed, or at least developed in an ancillary direction. This is normal, a combination of maturity and increasing self-awareness. Until my midthirties, I said I was extroverted, because I was socially competent and loved people. So confusing was my habit of dreading parties and avoiding small talk and hiding in bathroom stalls at large events *as the speaker*, I mistook it all as selfishness and vowed to do better. It wasn't until I read *Quiet: The Power of Introverts in a World That Can't Stop Talking* by Susan Cain that a lightbulb blazed to life above my head. I am not bad; I am a textbook introvert! I didn't have the language for that diagnosis earlier, but it has served me immensely since.

It takes a while to figure ourselves out, that's all. If you are young in this, keep going. If you are further along, don't be afraid to challenge an old paradigm when new internal evidence presents itself to the contrary. We must be kind to ourselves, patient in a way our future selves would insist upon. The tension, the stretch and pull, the doubt and questions—these are companions to this work.

Moving on to observable patterns. Sometimes our bodies and mouths and habits tell us who we are first. You are in a conversation in which your agreement is assumed, yet your neck becomes blotchy. You are an accountant who has filled ten notebooks with poetry. Ten times out of ten, you choose a funny movie over a dramatic one. You size up a room in two minutes flat and figure out who you can trust. You consistently throw out your plans in favor of spontaneous get-togethers. You have sixteen ideas for a new business. You keep getting in confrontations defending people even though you were never considered a challenger. Nine couples are now married because you set them up on their first date.

What do you keep doing? What do you keep saying? How do you consistently respond? What constantly sticks in your craw? What idea do you keep pushing? What thought do you keep thinking? When does your body tell you how you actually feel? Who do you keep agreeing with? What keeps giving you life? What keeps draining you dry? Where do you keep going, or to whom? What do your instincts and preferences and temperament and gut-checks show you?

Again, this identification is a sliding scale depending on how naturally self-aware you are. But even in the absence of intention, our interior mechanisms still tend to show themselves. Sometimes they come out of our mouths; other times they remain steadfastly in our thoughts. But they exist because we are who we are. Just pay attention. Maybe these consistent qualities aren't one-offs. Perhaps a reckoning is in order when you say, "You know what? I think this is who I actually am."

It took a combination of these first two components, enough lived years and observable patterns, added to the third, intentional investigation, before I stepped into my skin. Since I do not naturally self-assess, you must drag me to this task. But the very simple "extrovert or introvert" discovery was so monumental to my mental health, ultimately informing how I structured my life, that I knew there was great advantage to intentionally investigating my own wiring, not only for myself but my marriage, family, and career. This is not exhausting self-obsession nor a ploy to secure more "me time" or whatever the trendy phrase is. Rather, this self-awareness disrupts unhealthy patterns, instructs our decisions, strengthens our relationships, and illuminates our lanes. It is worth the effort.

Even though you and I are *obviously* unique snowflakes, distinct prizes in the universe, there is actually some science to personalities that researchers can wrangle into a quantified, testable format, says Simine Vazire, a psychology professor at the University of California, Davis. We have a variety of tools at our disposal here, none perfect but all useful: Myers Briggs, Strengths Finder, the Enneagram, Jung personality test, the Big Five, and plenty others. Critics of these inventories cite faulty self-reporting, human fluidity, and junk science as discrediting factors, and in some cases they may be right, but my experience with these tools has been overwhelmingly helpful. I consider none of the findings concrete, yet they throw on lights in the rooms we already occupy.

Personally, the tool that aided my interior work most profoundly was the Enneagram. I am only a user here, not an expert, so I will not spill much ink discussing its history and structure. I'll simply say that the Enneagram read me my own mail so accurately, I was afraid to discuss it publicly, because now you people know exactly what makes me tick. *They'll know my weak spots! They'll know how I'm gross sometimes! They'll know what motivates me!* How dare the Enneagram put our real selves on display for everyone to see. (One of its best features is not only showing us our best qualities but also revealing how we feel and act when disintegrating: *Look! Here you are at your absolute best! A created masterpiece and a joy to the world! And this is what you look like when you become a monster. Have a nice day.*)

For Enneagramateurs, I am a Three:

> Threes are self-assured, attractive, and charming. Ambitious, competent, and energetic, they can also be status-conscious and highly driven for advancement. They are diplomatic and

poised, but can also be overly concerned with their image and what others think of them. They typically have problems with workaholism and competitiveness. At their best: self-accepting, authentic, everything they seem to be—role models who inspire others.[3]

Cute. Would love to leave it at "at their best," but also there is this: "Fearing failure and humiliation, they can be exploitative and opportunistic, covetous of the success of others, and willing to do whatever it takes to preserve the illusion of their superiority." Precious.

In short, Threes can be gracious, authentic leaders building up the community to its highest ideals, and they can be jealous, competitive fakers who will stay on top at all costs. Threes want to be successful according to their niche cultural norms, and a bunch of them become pastors and authors . . . ahem. Examples include Oprah, Condoleeza Rice, and Reese Witherspoon. Yay! Also Bernie Madoff, O. J. Simpson, and Augustus Caesar, so. . . .

Any serious woman determined to own her inner workings must be prepared to identify both her inherent strengths and weaknesses. This is a terrible, terrible part of the work, and I do wish we could skip over it to the parts where we are incorruptible princess unicorns only capable of magic and light. If only everyone else would behave, then we wouldn't be forced to lose our shiz or commit tiny, tiny verbal crimes. It's not us! It's them! Alas, understanding how we are made on the inside includes the parts that are, um, less flattering.

Not only has the Enneagram helped me make sense of my interior life, but it has lent a great deal of strength to my marriage. Brandon is a Two, also called The Helper, and when I read what it looks like when a Three marries a Two, it was so accurate, it was spooky. Understanding his wiring shed some light on really old tension points. It helped me understand what was under some of his responses that have always perplexed me, especially in conflict, and gave me crystal-clear insight on how best to love him. It also outlined all the ways we are great together (we fit the exact profile of a Two guy married to a Three girl) with suggestions on how to communicate in each other's language and understand each other's motivations.

My assistant Amanda and I also shared our Enneagram findings with each other, and I immediately understood where I was failing her and how I could create a healthier work environment. She is a doggedly faithful Six, which means she will go all the way down with my ship. Loyalty is one of her top values. "Tell me more, not less" is her motto, because that signals trust. This was so useful because, as a Three, I value efficiency and bullet points; "Tell me less, not more" is my mantra. But, listen, no living person would suggest I lack words, so you want more of this? Pull up a chair, sister. I now send her long rants about our shared work life, she sends me numbered lists, and we live happily ever after.

If you'll allow one more layer: the Enneagram has been a profound spiritual development tool as well. Having spent half my life basically nervous around God and trying to please him with good behavior, my inner Three finally said: *Do you see what this is?* Afraid of failure, achievement oriented, wanting to appear good. I have both rightly and wrongly assessed God through my own internal compass. I falsely assigned some qualities to God that were really just an outcropping of my own fears. I envisioned a God based on my own image.

Unspooling that narrative is taking longer than I want, but I'm learning that he created us, as our Enneagram teachers say, *at our best.* He is not some version of my worst critic, the one I am always battling, but a loving creator proud of his kids. He is the best of all our qualities, not the worst.

Do the work to find out what your best looks like. Deep dive into your personality, motives, fears, qualities, tendencies—the landscape of your soul. Diagnostic tools are online, in books, illuminated by counselors. They are not prescriptive but rather descriptive, as human beings are not rigid. The Enneagram teachers say we have a bit of all nine types in us, so use these as tools, not templates.

Finally, since self-reporting can be admittedly unreliable, especially for those of us who don't instinctively self-assess, your very best people can usually confirm or deny your findings. They are often the truest mirror. They have seen you at your best and worst, through successes and failures, gains and losses, in front of the curtain and behind it, under pressure and on top of the world. They know.

I emailed the paragraph above (If I've done the work well . . .) to Brandon and asked, "I am writing through a piece in the book about self-identification and discovering a strong internal compass. This is what I said about myself. Is this right? Is this how I am perceived and experienced? Does this feel like an accurate assessment?" We have been married twenty-five years, birthed and adopted five kids, and weathered one million storms. He has seen it all. He is my biggest fan and also isn't buying my crap. I can't Instagram filter my way out of the real story with a person I have been married to well over half my life.

His response was classic Brandon identifying classic Jen: "First, I appreciate you asking me. I know that was risky. Second, I do think this is a fair and accurate assessment. You clearly state what you do and how you do it. You are all these things: justice oriented, funny, tender, ambitious, assertive, etc. If you're really wanting to go deeper to help people out with discovery you should discuss the 'why' behind it. That's your Enneagram stuff. Why don't you like showing that you can be tender? Why are you conflicted? Why are

you guarded? Those are the things that help people truly understand their internal compass and natural responses."

What did I tell you? You can see the spots I am frustrating. I am
not easily vulnerable, don't talk about my insides enough, and tend
to be guarded even inside my own marriage. Brandon, on the other
hand, is (sometimes painfully) transparent, loves to talk about his
feelings, and would love to talk more about mine. Yay! Fun! He
confirmed my best qualities while honing in on the ways I still tend
to hide. Dammit.

My friends are excellent character witnesses too. An Enneagram
teacher recently suggested that I might be an Eight instead of a
Three, and I sat deeply with that. I examined the descriptions and
searched internally for evidence, as an Eight and Three are both
powerful personality types with some crossover. I relate to much
of the Eight's determination but could *not* identify with the shadow
side (ruthless, combative, intentionally intimidating), so I asked
my friends, who always have permission to tell me the truth, "Do
you ever experience me like this?" They categorically said no. And
they were right. That is not the way I disintegrate, but I checked
any blind spots just in case. Our best people know. (One of my girlfriends said, "No, but I have absolutely experienced you as the dark
side of a Three." THANK YOU FOR GOING BEYOND THE
QUESTION I ASKED, JENNY.)

Our closest people can correct us when we think too high and
too low of ourselves, because we tend to inflate both. I am not as
good as my ego suggests and not as bad as my conscience admon-
ishes. After carefully examining our lived experiences, observable
patterns, and personality inventories, we can present our findings to the ones who love us best and know us most, and if we've
approached the work with sincerity and humility, they will likely
confirm our conclusions and even fine-tune the story a bit.

Who you are matters. Your soul is cause for great delight.

There is freedom in this discovery and absolute liberation in its ownership. When who you are on the inside matches the outside, you are ready for everything else.

Embrace your rational, principled, restrained self.

Or your demonstrative, generous, service-minded self.

Or your sensitive, expressive, creative self.

Or your intense, perceptive, cerebral self.

Engaging, responsible, loyal.

Fun-loving, spontaneous, extroverted.

Powerful, ambitious, confident.

Easy-going, agreeable, gentle.

Spicy, confrontational, bold.

Private, careful, quiet.

Tender, emotional, graceful.

Wild, silly, outrageous.

There is so much good handwoven into every human person. Such beauty. So many gifts to be spilled generously onto the rest of us. We must show up truthfully, because it is in the diversity of our souls this world receives all it needs. We do not need you to be like your neighbor; we already have her. We need you, not for what you do but who you are. Please be her. Please do not shrink or twist or lie or buckle. Please do not mislabel your beautiful inmost being as too weak, too strong, too little, too much. Stop apologizing. Stop shape-shifting. Do the work and show up for your life, because you are the only one who can live it, and the rest of us need you.

2

I AM EXACTLY ENOUGH

At the beginning of my public career, I was invited to deliver the Sunday morning sermon at a very large, very traditional church as a guest preacher. I was young in my field, sprouting little wings, ready to fly. This invitation was outrageously flattering and alternatively terrifying. I'd not yet preached on this scale and definitely not in front of that many men. I was developing my chops in the Lady Spaces, so this felt like being promoted to Big Church. I worked on that sermon like it was my doctoral thesis. I had the minor prophets, Mother Mary, the church grandmas, and Jesus of Nazareth on my personal prayer team. I spent one hundred dollars we didn't have on an outfit, because I love the Lord but *I come correct.*

As I sat on the front row nervously shuffling through my notes, preparing for my first moment as a spiritual authority in such a legitimate space, the pastor introduced me to his congregation: "Ladies, you are in for a real treat today. Jen is here to share some stories with you, and I think you'll be tickled. And men? We will just peek over their shoulders this morning until we resume our sermon series next week."

What.

In.

The.

Actual.

Hell.

I burned with humiliation from the top of my skull to the soles of my fancy new shoes. I fully expected him to pat me on the head when I reached the stage. I thought I was invited to preach to the church, not tell some cute stories to the gals while the men looked on condescendingly, apparently unable to learn from a woman. I wasn't prepared for the misogyny, a word I didn't know back then but whose effects I felt acutely. I also later discovered they paid my male colleague *twenty-five hundred dollars* to guest preach a sermon in the same series; I got a check for one hundred dollars and paid my own way to get there.

Believe me, I got the message: *you deserve less authority, less credit, less respect, and less compensation, so be sure to take up less space.* And shrink I did. It was all so embarrassing; I didn't recognize the small box reserved for me until I showed up expecting to fill the whole room.

This culture is rabid to tell women how much oxygen they can use, space they can take, tables they can join, opinions they are allowed. Code words abound to signal when a woman has stepped too far: *hysterical, bitchy, bossy, aggressive.* (The man versions of these words are: *energetic, strong, decisive, assertive,* because "bossy men" are just called "leaders.") Women have always struggled for a credible place at the table.

So it is that reporters declare Yahoo CEO Marissa Mayer "crazy" and "too tough," while Amazon's Jeff Bezos is "audacious" and "determined," a "rare leader who obsesses over finding small improvements." (In female terms: *micromanager.*) According to *The New York Times,* Justice Sonia Sotomayor "has a blunt and even testy side," while Antonin Scalia is "colorful" and "provocative."[1]

From an early age, girls are taught overtly and subtly to contain and defer, while the boys are encouraged to expand and assert. We overapologize. We shrug and accommodate. Women cede the microphone to less capable people, because we are socialized to grow inward while men are conditioned to grow outward. Women often believe that rather than simply taking up the right amount of space they are *displacing* others with their presence, and how dare they.

Psychotherapist Kimberly Key wrote,

> Part of the difficulty is that men are more wired to be hierarchical and see things in win-lose scenarios. . . . Women, on the other hand, are more hard-wired to be more multitasking and collaborative and seek win-win solutions. . . . The wonderful thing in our evolution and growth is that gender norms are changing a bit and with increasing role-reversals, a bigger bridge between the sexes is built. Even so, the greater majority of men and women reveal pretty entrenched male-female neurological patterning.[2]

It is worth noting that women are often the greatest offenders against other women here. With patriarchy internalized, our own community penalizes one another for breaking gender norms. I have taken up way too much space for some women. They are among my most severe critics, and they usually reach for Christian tropes to shrink me down to size: *this is why women shouldn't preach, you are a false teacher, you just love the world.* (Side note: Yes, I do love the world. Jesus loved the world, which is why he came.)

I sometimes check my critics' online bios to determine if I should engage in good faith, and when the comment is especially mean-spirited, nine times out of ten the woman's moniker is "Daughter of the King." The King's daughters are THE WORST. I only want to hang out with the King's kitchen staff, because his internet daughters are mean as the Devil's hell.

Ironically, similar pressure is often placed on women who are content behind the scenes or happy with the simple life they love: *Oh, you're just a stay-at-home mom? You only work part-time? You still live in your hometown? You let him/her/them be in charge? You should speak up more often. You should go for more. You should stake your claim. You should increase your goals.* Where the conspicuous leaders are called power-hungry bitches, these women are called weak-willed doormats, meek pushovers who settled for less. And, just like that, the message is flipped: *you don't take up* enough *space.*

Hell, there is a whole industry built on telling us we should be more. That what we have isn't enough, what we love is too ordinary, how we live is pedestrian. Contentment is rebranded as mediocrity. We digest this idea that, by pulling a few levers, we could (and should!) transform our lives into a new, shinier version, because unless we are daily reaching for the stars, we are living like plebeians and bringing unhappiness upon our dumb little lives.

My dear friend Shannan Martin wrote, in *The Ministry of Ordinary Places,*

> I prefer to be seen as special. Unique. Ordinary places and average people remind me of everything I'm pretending not to be. The worst part about this fruitless mission to outrun ordinary is that sometimes it kind of works. Sometimes, the applause is loud enough to drown out the sound of our souls collapsing under the weight of a burden we were never meant to carry. All the while, we're peering out our windows, waiting to be seen for

exactly who we are. We're walking sidewalks and cereal aisles, longing for the assurance that we have something to offer, we are worthy of connection and love.[3]

We are way too much.

We are way too mediocre.

We are way too small.

Women are expected to thread this impossible needle of being just enough for whomever is asking, a Goldilocks prototype who always picks the right chair. We are expected to push the needle but not too far, challenge the status quo but not too dramatically, and lead in strength but not if it makes someone uncomfortable.

Hold my earrings!

While it is true that women have historically been shrink-wrapped into a tidier version of traditional domesticity, it is also true that there is no one-size-fits-all message for how much space women should take up. That's just silly. Any notion that we should shrink or expand on demand to meet some prototype of empowerment (either less or more) harms the community of women immeasurably.

To those wired to lead and live large—let's call them Mega Women—telling them to be smaller is absurd. Are we going to call up Oprah and Kamala and Reese and Michelle O and Malala and Tina and Beth and tell them their power is outsized? That they missed the meeting on appropriate lady rules and should tone it down? I pity the misguided soul that attempts to tether Shonda Rhimes. Some women were meant for bigger spaces, because they were born with big personalities, big ideas, and big capacity. Where would we be if Mega Women hadn't powered through opposition to build and create, lead and influence, disrupt and reform? What world would we live in if they didn't push past boundaries for more? One without *Scandal* and *Bossypants* and the right to vote and preach, I'll tell you that right now. That world would be a disaster; we are all beneficiaries of Mega Women and their Mega Lives.

What about the opposite end of the spectrum? To the women thriving in a quiet, private life, let's say Modest Women, insisting they loom larger is preposterous. Why should they? Who said the Mega Women are the only ones who register? Why should our most gentle, behind-the-scenes women be peer pressured into expansive spaces they don't want to fill? We've conflated "big" with "important," but that is a false equivalency. There isn't a person or community on earth that hasn't been nurtured by Modest Women who occupy humble spaces, supporting their people in ways that may be hidden to the watching eye but run deep as the ocean in their actual lives. The spotlight has corrosive powers, and these women avoid its contamination and inject our culture with inordinate amounts of grace. Modest Women have been some of the most impactful mentors in my life. Their influence might not roar, but it is no less powerful.

How about somewhere between the two? To the women perfectly, absolutely content with what they have and where they are, right in the pocket in the middle of the dial—Mezzo Women, we'll say—calling them mediocre is ludicrous. Who decided everyday contentment is lacking? Why does leadership have to look big and loud? Frankly, intermediators are doing a wonderful service to the world right now. I see them acting beautifully as bridge builders, peacemakers, compromise-brokers, and soothers. They are actively leading in their spheres, raising their voices at their volume and in their way. They are anchored in their communities and deeply in tune with their neighbors. They are role models combatting the insatiability of a "more is better" culture. Where would we be if Mezzo Women hadn't planted roots and held their communities together? What world would we live in if they didn't temper the alpha culture with reason and dialogue? Mezzo Women are the reason we still have a sense of home, connection, comfort. How dare anyone convince them to be dissatisfied with their lives.

The key to health here is knowing who *you* are, how *you* were formed, and in what space *you* thrive. There is no superior volume to aim for—we are in great need of Mega, Mezzo, and Modest Women—rather, determine your proper container. We wobble when pressured to dial up or down against our makeup. To a Mezzo Woman, there is nothing more exhausting than being urged to act bigger, reach higher, live bigger. Let her live, Universe! And you can try to tell a Mega Woman to shrink it down, but you better duck. And I guess insisting that our Modest Women act dominant is our way to destroy their perfectly engineered souls? I have always resisted one-size-fits-all instruction here, because women take up different amounts of space based on their inherent design, preferences, and personalities.

My agenda is not for all women to take up more space.

I want you to say confidently, "I take up the *right amount* of space."

I'm pretty Mega with a dose of Mezzo, so I am usually urged to diminish or occasionally expand, depending on the eye of the beholder. On August 7, 1974, I was born with big dreams, big ideas, and big opinions. I was a Mega Toddler who needed a Blackberry and a full-time assistant. This is uncontested data. I am comfortable taking up a lot of space, because all this communiqué needs somewhere to go. I require a big container, or I will spill out on everyone around me like a fifth-grade volcano science project. I have ideas! Words! Feelings! I would also like to be in charge! I am very interested in taking this hill! We march at dawn! This is why I can digest counsel to *ramp it up* easier than *settle down*. It is in keeping with how I am wired. (Note to self: Speak to counselor about historic struggle with church definition of womanhood. Could be related. Maybe not a mystery.)

Let's talk about you. I suspect you have experienced frustration if you've been urged to fill the wrong container. Think through leaders you follow, in real life and online. If their messaging consistently makes you feel either hamstrung or exhausted, could it be they are leading out of their personal volume but it doesn't match yours? Or maybe it is your boss, coworker, employee, or friend. People typically engage from their own capacity and its corresponding practices, which is why I opened this chapter with a story as a Mega forced to deflate, then spent one thousand words lamenting the muzzling of women before turning to you like, "Oh. Hi. I didn't see you there."

Even as a big-space type, I have my limits. I follow a couple of influencers whose every post is about trying harder, becoming better, dreaming bigger, and running faster. Look, I love to try, become, dream, and run (metaphorically, omg), but even I finally throw my hands up and scream, "NOPE. TODAY I WILL LIE ON THE COUCH AND WATCH FOOTBALL AND EAT CHIPS. The only dream I will have today is during my nap." I can imagine how draining this do-more tidal wave is for the lower-key Mezzos and Modests. However, it has an unbelievably positive effect on most Megas.

Maybe you need a big container to hold all your stuffings, but your community or work environment or home life prefers less volume. Megas and high-octane Mezzos famously push the envelope in traditional spaces that venerate homogeny, patriarchy, politeness, or the status quo. Shouldering the inevitable disapproval is so discouraging. The only way to shove a square peg in a round hole is to lose the edges, and the big-space types were born with edges.

There is nothing more life-giving than an environment that matches your volume. It is hard to put a price on being seen and valued as you are. When you don't have to ratchet down or falsely inflate but are welcomed with your contents exactly intact, this is when we thrive. I operate in several of these environments, and my big feelings (would I have any other kind?) explode with gratitude. I was born to parents who still believe we were all mislabeled prodigies, I married a man who thinks I should run the country, and I lead in a church that champions lady preachers. My chosen environment never asks me to simmer down.

Listen, there is nothing wrong with how much space you are geared to take up. There is not a superior way to be, regardless of what messages you are picking up in the atmosphere. You do not need to be more or less; what matters is decoding what container you flourish in. This is your work, your verdict, and your line to hold. It is upon you to insist on your space, even when it is discouraged or belittled.

And here you may need some courage.

When the command aimed at women is "be less," the tactics include insulting, condescending, bullying, and manipulating. The goal is to make you shrink, so the maneuver will attempt to make you feel small. Your competence will be challenged, your authority dismissed, your experience questioned, your voice silenced. The endgame is your feeling deflated enough to bench yourself. Happens all the time. This coercion can occur inside a marriage, extended family, career, church, friendship, or any community. With women having already internalized a lifetime of messages that they are too much, it doesn't take much browbeating to reinforce the memo.

You are not required to justify your space nor hustle for approval. If someone wants you to be smaller, that is their problem, not yours. You do not need to offer a lengthy defense of your credentials or opinions. An assertive woman will always face resistance, if not early on, eventually. Some potential responses that don't include your dancing like a monkey for permission:

I am more than capable for this task/work/position/
    responsibility.
I am not asking for your permission.
I am not asking for your approval.
I am not asking for your opinion.
I appreciate your position here, but I still disagree.
I will not be bullied out of this (or into this).
I've done the work and made my decision.
I will lead/execute/create in my way.

You choose to wither on command or not. Regardless of how fierce the opposition, it is your decision to own your space or concede it. Never does this require hysterics or rudeness, which typically weaken your position even as those exact tactics are used against you, because #doublestandard. Rather, it requires sturdy confidence: I take up the right amount of space here. The end.

I know a thing or two about standing your ground. I could fill every page of this book with correspondence meant to terrify me into submission, ranging from "your husband needs to get you in check" to "this is why mommy bloggers shouldn't be given laptops" to "the term *sit down and shut up* was literally created for women like you." I once confronted an evangelical professor online for his outrageous assertion that providing basic protections for LGBTQ employees at an international nonprofit that has served the world's poor for decades signaled "the collapse of Christianity." At the time, I was still on the payroll of a conservative publishing house, and my editor called me, desperately whispering, "I am in a staff meeting, and everyone is freaking out about your blog! It is the subject of the whole meeting!" I literally blinked a few times into my phone and said, "And?" Their male authors criticized countless folks online and in their books, but they were stymied by a female challenger. They were not at all offended that this professor (and in-house author!) *denied the salvation* of the organization's president but only with my rebuttal. WHATEVER SHALL WE DO WHEN A LADY WRITER CALLS OUT ONE OF OUR BROS? Good reader, I wondered if we would be able to collaborate anymore. (Narrator's voice: They were unable to collaborate anymore.)

When people tell you to sit down and shut up, you don't have to. I cannot make this any simpler. You can resist bullcrap and live to tell. What a world! They can't kill you! You are not required to depreciate so others can continue to take up more than their allotment. The status quo is counting on your submission, but you do not have to bow down.

This will create tension, but I'm convinced a tension-free culture is a dangerous one. Tension can be defined as the act of stretching or the state of being stretched. This practice is imperative to a healthy ethos. Folks have stretched me without mercy in the last decade, and I am categorically better for it. You will feel the stretch, you will cause the stretch in others, and this is called growing. If no one injects tension into the atmosphere, we will always default to existing power structures that operate beautifully as long as no one puts any pressure on them.

Inversely, when the command aimed at women is "be more," the tactics include patronizing, shaming, mocking, and coercing. The goal is to make you expand, so the maneuver, ironically, is also to make you feel small. Your goals are too pedestrian, your presence too inconsequential, your performance lacking. The endgame is you feeling ashamed enough to try and *Be More*. Happens all the time. Having already internalized a lifetime of messages that women are not enough, it takes very little shaming to affirm what we suspected: we are somehow failing. This dynamic can also incur inside a marriage, extended family, career, church, friendship, or any community.

You are not required to justify your space nor hustle for approval either. If someone wants you to loom larger, that is their problem, not yours. You do not need to offer a lengthy defense of your credentials or opinions. Just like the assertive woman, a reserved woman faces resistance too. Some responses that don't require your dancing like a monkey for approval:

I am enough here.
I am content with who I am.
I am content with what I have.
I am content with how I live.
I hear your opinion, but I don't share it.
I will not be bullied into this.
I will lead/execute/create in my own way.

Holding your space against outside pressure to be more is no different than those urged to be less. This is yours to protect. If someone wants you to be bigger by suggesting that you are too small, that is shame-based manipulation and you should resist it fiercely. In owning your space, there is no need to reach for the tools of dominance—aggression, arguing, offensiveness—but rather sturdy confidence: *I take up the right amount of space here. The end.*

There is not a woman alive who hasn't been told she was not doing enough, not achieving enough, not striving enough, not enough period. Ironically, our culture wants us to be more in certain categories but absolutely less in others. This is a moving target depending on group norms, geography, and communal expectations. It takes just as much courage to resist this damaging messaging, which is tricky because the mean voice is often *our own.* We absorb the cultural criterion that prioritizes the loudest voices in the room, and it is a short leap to incorporate the message: more is better.

More is not better.

This is a lie, pure and simple. Regardless of how much value is assigned to the More Folks, forceful is not inherently better than gentle, assertive is not automatically better than conciliatory, and highly visible is not more important than discreet. I cannot imagine a more debased world than every human adjusting his or her internal compass to become the biggest dog in the pound. Our cultural health depends on the checks and balances of various volumes. We temper one another in dazzling ways. The Megas sometimes rally the Mezzos and Modests toward healthy expansion, and the Modests and Mezzos teach the Megas restraint and grace. We are good for each other. We round out our communities and protect them from one-note sameness.

We need more women comfortable in their own skin. The constant scurrying up and down the scales to hit some imaginary target is exhausting. Know who you are, know how you thrive, know your own volume, and live unapologetically in that lane. Hold your territory. As much as it depends on you, weed out the voices insisting you become more or less; don't be a glutton for your own punishment.

Before closing out this chapter, I want to acknowledge the fluidity of these categories I made up with clever alliteration (you can pry literary devices out of my cold, dead hands, including this delicious parenthetical thought, because I have lots to say about the thing I am already saying): sometimes the shyest, quietest, most demure woman is the biggest Mega in the room. Or the wordy lady taking up all the oxygen deeply craves a Modest life. Mezzos can go any which way and constantly surprise people.

I call as my witness Ruth Bader Ginsberg, who appears to be a tiny, meek granny wearing white gloves, the quietest person in the room, but is actually a twenty-five-year Supreme Court Justice, a pioneering attorney and judge for civil and equal rights, maybe the most important feminist of our time. You had to lean all the way in to hear her quiet little voice quote Sarah Grimke in her first argument before the Supreme Court in 1972: "I ask no favors for my sex. All I ask of our brethren is that they will take their feet from off our necks." OKAY, QUEEN. Come through, RBG!

I also want to acknowledge that sometimes we ratchet up or down for a specific task. There comes a moment when a deeply private person inclined toward prudence steps into the spotlight because justice or passion or necessity compels her. My restrained mom, the only temperate member of our family, rises up in absolute authority about once every three years over something important to her, and it shocks and delights us every time. We mustn't blame our detrimental silence on tender personalities, nor make apologies for claiming greater space though it isn't our custom. We may have our norms, but no one is excluded (or exempted) from turning up the mic sometimes. Many of our greatest advocates jumped in from the sidelines driven by conviction.

Similarly, wisdom insists that even the loudest trumpet in the band should sometimes sit quietly and learn from the experts, the experienced, and the marginalized. Pity the person who considers her voice the most important resource in every room. There is a time to be smaller or even take an entire season to rest, regroup, recover, renew. Three years ago, I took a whole year off: no speaking, no traveling, very little writing, quieter in all my roles. Having operated with my foot on the gas for fifteen years in the public eye, I needed a minute to remember who I was, what mattered, and why I serve. I cannot teach a good story if I am not living one. Did I worry about scarcity as if it would all be gone when I came back? I sure did, and I was wrong. There is a season for smaller, simpler, softer, and it does not threaten our normal capacity.

Here is the bottom line: you are well put together exactly how you are. You may be your sister's keeper, but you are not her copy. Don't look sideways. Don't look to media. Don't look to your group's norms. Don't look to some reduced definition of womanhood or feminism. Whatever container you naturally fill *is the perfect one.* You take up the right amount of space. So take it up.

And listen here: this does not mean you no longer make room for others. Scarcity is actually what drives us to claim too much or too little, this suspicion that there is not enough to go around so we better either gobble up all we can or throw in the towel. I am solidly on record here: this is some Grade A horsecrap.

We are free to exist on this planet in the ways we flourish, because there is an abundance of everything: joy, talent, love, dreams, hope, goodness, triumph, creativity, delight. Every one of these is a renewable resource. Never, not for one day, has there not been enough. Someone else's space does not diminish yours. You are entirely free to celebrate your sisters, to pull up more chairs to the table, to lead, to learn, to cheer them on, to push them forward, to share your influence. You are not threatened; therefore, you do not need to be a threat.

There is room for you, just the right amount. There is room for others, just the right amounts. There is an endless supply of portions. Settle right into your skin, dear one. What a great delight you are. Be content and proud of your range, the lane you thrive in, the capacity in which you blossom.

This King's kitchen staffer is thrilled to be your sister.

3

I AM STRONG IN MY BODY

When I was in elementary school, I would ball up my dad's tube socks inside a tank top and practice my budding (*sic*) Madonna personality in the mirror, admiring my lumpy, irregularly shaped sock breasts and mentally preparing for the inevitable windfall I'd experience once I got my grown-up bod. If my dad's softball socks were any indicator, I was heading for some serious modeling opportunities once I could grow out my home perm and minimize my horse teeth. I'd seen my future, and it looked like Cindy Crawford's second cousin.

As a high school cheerleader (this is so obviously on brand), I lamented my oafish, whale-like body that eventually showed up. Never the tiny flyer but the hulking base, I was basically fit for the offensive line or, at best, the roller derby. I'd stare at my thighs and will them to be thinner, shocked at my capacity for childhood obesity. Was it something with my thyroid? Was it my daily lunch of Jolly Ranchers Fire Stix? Would Buffalo Bill have targeted me for his skin costume because of my ample brawn? (*Silence of the Lambs* was the leading cause of my sophomore-year trauma.) It seemed clear that the 1990 Cheerleading Base Community was in danger, and we should switch to Tab simply to save our lives. I was 5 feet, 8 inches and 130 pounds. I wore a size six.

When I was finally a grown lady with all her faculties in place, I drank nothing but water spiked with cayenne and lemon for five days, because the internet said this was a smart way to fit back into your jeans. As it turned out, it was a good way to get diarrhea, which *will* eventually get you into your pants if you don't mind a mild case of dehydration. I also once paid American dollars for someone to weigh me weekly after buying their expensive, garbage, processed food with the cheery assurance that I could enjoy "unlimited lettuce" outside of their Fudgy Peanut Butter Crunch Bar and Cheddar Cheese and Bacon–Flavored Omelet Mix (just add water!). When I asked if I could just eat an egg instead, the consultant stared at me like I'd requested one of her kidneys without anesthesia. I'm not Hannibal Lector! I just want an egg!

Women have waged a long, brutal war against their bodies. We've squared off in our corners, determined to make our bodies smaller and our ages indiscernible. It is a scorched-earth, take-no-prisoners brawl, and, if I'm reading the room right, it is breaking our hearts. If I had every second back that I've spent thinking about my weight and age, my belly and my crow's feet, I could have cured cancer with all the extra time—if only I understood molecular research and/or science.

Springboarding off the last chapter, when it comes to our bodies, the cultural message is positively clear: be less. Literally take up less space with your flesh and bones and occupy fewer years on the calendar, because we like our ladies skinny and young-looking (not young-acting or, you know, actually young). Automatic favor is assigned to women who fit the criteria, so the rest of us detox and peel and wrap and laser and purge and fast, attempting to shed pounds and years off our wild and precious lives.

A moment of transparency: as I scan the twelve chapters I am writing, this is the main area where I still feel suffocated. I want to write from a place of strength, but the truth is I do not yet possess a healthy body image. I've breathed the toxic air of extreme dieting, unrealistic goals, media misrepresentation, and self-loathing for too long. I haven't experienced another way. The ideal body type became crystal clear to me before I exited elementary school. Every movie, magazine, commercial, TV show, ad, marketing campaign, product, endorsement, and punch line has taught me the score for forty-five years: model-thin is the path to happiness. Even as I type that line, I still kind of believe it. Something in me maintains that pulling on a tiny pair of "junior jeans" will usher me into not just contentment but outright joy. The rot has truly set.

So, if I may be your sister in this space, I would love to find our way out of this chronic unhappiness. It steals too much. And I tread carefully, as this is a complex conversation with many layers. For the purposes of this section, I am not addressing life-threatening eating disorders or weight-related health problems. Those are very real concerns that require attention and medical care and treatment. Pushing our bodies to extremes can shorten our lives. There are legitimate reasons to focus all our energy on getting healthy. And there is not a single thing wrong with exercise, healthy eating, and fitness; none of that indicates mania or that you are easily manipulated. My seventy-two-year-old dad runs four miles a day and therefore will probably live to be 117, which is fabulous because we will not have to fight over who gets his Corvette since we will all be too old to drive.

But for women who waste untold emotional energy chasing an impossible ideal, who harm ourselves with junk diets and pills to outrun the normal, human body we are walking around in, we have to deboard this crazy train. Don't you want to? Wouldn't it be a relief to cast off the self-loathing and free up the mental space? While most of our true interior identity needs courage to live openly on the outside, in this case, our exterior is fighting for a kinder home inside our minds. The container carrying us through life is simply asking to be loved instead of hated.

Let's get clear: this issue starts when we're super young. Body negativity does not strangely materialize in adulthood, stealing whatever earnest innocence we enjoyed as girls. One study reports that, at age thirteen, 53 percent of American girls are "unhappy with their bodies." This grows to 78 percent by the time girls reach seventeen.[1] When researchers followed a group of 496 adolescent girls for eight years until they were twenty, they found 5.2 percent of the girls met criteria for anorexia, bulimia, or binge-eating disorder. When the researchers included nonspecific eating-disorder symptoms, 13.2 percent of the girls qualified, which means an unsettling number of young women meet clinical criteria for a pathological relationship with food and self-image. And then there's this, which is so sobering: more than one-half of teenage girls and nearly one-third of teenage boys practice unhealthy weight control behaviors like skipping meals, fasting, smoking cigarettes, vomiting, and taking laxatives.[2]

> Seventy-eight percent of our teen girls are unhappy with
> their young, beautiful bodies.
> Thirteen percent of them suffer from eating disorders.
> More than 50 percent of them try to lose weight by starving
> or puking.

We are just these girls grown up. I still meet two of those three data points. It is simple: disordered thinking leads to disordered eating. Young girls are thinking terribly about their bodies, and they never stop until one day they are forty-five years old and writing a chapter about it. Listen, if you struggle here, you are not self-obsessed, uniquely unhappy, or weak-willed; you are the intended result of an industry devised to make you feel bad about yourself so it can capitalize on your inevitable despair. We didn't even know crow's feet were a *catastrophe* until Neutrogena told us they were (with an easy solution to fix them for $29.99!).

You are not alone and not crazy. If you are plagued by dark thoughts about your body, it is because you've been targeted for a message since you were little, and you received it. Simple as that. So, if there is no disruption in the way we perceive our bodies, no concerted effort to rewire our ideals, we will not miraculously escape this poisonous mental loop just because we hit adulthood.

Let's start where it starts: in our minds. Beginning with this key message delivered through every possible channel: *This is what pretty looks like.* You already know what it is. We all do. We are keenly aware of the beauty standards heralded by all. Which is why a lady like me in her midforties who has birthed three children and raised five believes she should look like a sorority girl who was in middle school six years ago. I got the hair memo, the skin memo, the thigh-gap memo, the fashion memo, the boob memo, the BMI memo. Message received, Beauty Industry.

It's worth noting that standardized beauty has always been a shifting target. Sure, we see what pretty looks like, but that is only what pretty looks like *right now* (and also *right here*; for the Masai tribe in Kenya, a woman's beauty is heightened by how elongated her earlobes have become, so I am obviously applying for a visa). Hell, this criteria has shifted in our own lifetime, and yet, rather than exposing it as a fraud, we adjust our sails and chase the next iteration of beautiful. Let's trace standardized beauty through its cycles as idealized in literature, art, advertising, and documented cultural norms:

ANCIENT GREECE (500–300 BC): plump, full-bodied, light skinned.

HAN DYNASTY (206 BC–AD 220): slim waist, pale skin, large eyes, small feet.

ITALIAN RENAISSANCE (1400–1700): ample bosom, rounded stomach, full hips, fair skin.

VICTORIAN ENGLAND (1837–1901): desirably plump, full-figured, cinched waist (corset generation).

Closer in to our Western-centric phases:

ROARING TWENTIES (1920s): flat chest, downplayed waist, bobbed hair, boyish figure.

GOLDEN AGE OF HOLLYWOOD (1930s–1950s): curves, hourglass figure, large breasts, slim waist (pin-up girls).

SWINGING SIXTIES (1960s): willowy, thin, long slim legs, adolescent physique.

SUPERMODEL ERA (1980s): athletic, svelte but curvy, tall, toned arms (widespread obsession with exercise).

HEROIN CHIC (1990s): waifish, extremely thin, translucent skin, androgynous.

POSTMODERN BEAUTY (2000s–today): flat stomach, "healthy" skinny, tan, large breasts and butt, thigh gap.[3]

Um, okay.

And maybe I'm just bitter, but today's look du jour is legitimately absurd. My patroness Tina Fey put it like this in *Bossypants*:

Now every girl is expected to have Caucasian blue eyes, full Spanish lips, a classic button nose, hairless Asian skin with a California tan, a Jamaican dance hall ass, long Swedish legs, small Japanese feet, the abs of a lesbian gym owner, the hips of a nine-year-old boy, the arms of Michelle Obama, and doll tits.[4]

Sing it, sister. I would've been a prime piece of ribeye in Victorian England, but none of us stand a chance against the carefully engineered bodies of the Kardashians.

Perhaps we can quit drinking this Kool-Aid. Fact: I am 5 feet, 8 inches and from a family of big folk. We just aren't little people. I can abuse this container all I want, but I will never fit the suggested template. Unless you are the 1 percent of women born like that, you probably won't either. The rest of us are tall and short; curvy and stick straight; athletic and bony; big boobed and flat chested; apples, pears, and carrots; young, middle-aged, and seasoned— lovely all. The notion that our bodies should be measured against one standardized ideal is as ludicrous as our personalities adjusting to one standardized ideal.

Ironically, I can easily apply this freedom to you. I regularly marvel at the beauty of women outside the conventional checklist. And I mean it. This feels crystal clear to me when it comes to you, when it comes to my daughters and their friends, women I admire, international women, those twenty or forty years ahead of me. I do not apply the impossible rules to anyone but myself. Is this the hardest frontier?

When my doctor said my ideal weight was fifteen to twenty-five pounds above my "goal weight," I thought she was trolling me. It is a number I've held ransom for two decades. When I pushed back, she asked, "Where did you get such a low number? You would have to eat seven hundred calories a day to maintain that and sleep twelve hours a day to conserve energy, you know, due to the starvation." Good reader, I was sincerely shocked. It was like my doctor had never read a copy of *Elle* in her life. I honestly believed I had a reasonable goal for a normal weight. This is, as the experts describe, disordered thinking. I will never hit that silly number to match some glorified size, but it sure has made me unhappy trying.

Body ideals, like everything else in pop culture, are a trend. They aren't real. They are invented, then exploited by billion-dollar industries that profit from our self-loathing to abuse our bodies into shapes and sizes they were never designed to be. I have bad news for the women who purchased butt implants recently: the next trend will probably be Second-Grade Boy/Alien and your new round butts will need to be vacuumed out and repurposed into feet implants. (I am attempting to be a trendsetter and to elevate my personal traits.)

And that brings us to those billion-dollar industries. Girls, we've been losing this game for a long time. In fact, as slender bodies started to appear in magazines in the mid-1920s, an epidemic of eating disorders spiked among young women. "The highest reported prevalence of disordered eating occurred during the 1920s and 1980s, the two periods during which the 'ideal woman' was thinnest in US history," researchers wrote in the *Journal of Communication*. The bust-to-waist ratios among women featured in *Vogue* and *Ladies Home Journal* dwindled by about 60 percent between 1901 and 1925, according to a study published in the journal *Sex Roles*.[5]

This makes me want to fight someone. I realize much ink has been spilled about media's effect on our body image, but the truth is, it affects our actual health and happiness. It sends us down crazy rabbit holes of manic dieting and guilty binging. It causes spikes in eating disorders and social dysfunction; almost eight in ten girls (79 percent) and even more women (85 percent) admit to opting out of important events because they don't like how they look.[6] We spend billions of dollars on magic products guaranteed to help us lose dangerous amounts of weight in the shortest period of time. Every company has miraculously found The Thing—forget that their findings all contradict one another based on their own personal junk science. They have us by the throat. They know it. They know what levers to pull so we will open our wallets to their quick fixes.

We live in the perfect storm for body negativity to sail right off the edge of the map. Never in history have we had so many platforms on which to compare ourselves and such an unprecedented number of women to use as the template. In earlier societies, women had a very small pool, a genuine cross-section of features and body types. Today, the access to high concentrations of narrowly beautiful women creates a false standard. While a person previously might encounter one or two prescriptively gorgeous women in her lifetime, we are inundated with images today suggesting they are ubiquitous. We have the 1 percent of today's favorite type in our faces at all times on all platforms. We will likely be unpacking the social media effect on the human psyche for centuries.

What would have to happen for us to honor our bodies? What is the opposite approach from this toxic cycle of comparison, impossible standards, shame, and self-harm? What might it look like if a generation of women started celebrating their outsides on their insides? Is there a possible path from here to there? Because the chasm is wide, and who do we think is coming to our aid? The diet industry? Hollywood? Fashion culture? The beauty enterprise? They have nothing to gain if women refuse to hate their bodies. They are not our allies, no matter how much they profess to love women. We represent two key words to them: dollar signs. Get it straight.

So here, grab my hand. Let's walk away from our screens and cover models and chemical peels and A-listers and meal-replacement shakes and go outside. Let's sit on the porch where sanity lives and talk about what is real. In her book *Mothers, Daughters, and Body Image*, my friend Hillary McBride suggests calling our bodies "she" or "her"—a marked difference from "it," as if she isn't an integrated part of our whole being: "We often forget that mind and body are actually both equally *us*."[7] Your character and soul, intelligence and creativity, love and experiences, goodness and talents, your bright and lovely self are entwined with your body, and she has delivered the whole of you to this very day. What a partner! She has been a home for your smartest ideas, your triumphant spirit, your best jokes. You haven't gotten anywhere you've ever gone without her. She has served you well.

Your body walked with you all the way through childhood—climbed the trees and rode the bikes and danced the ballet steps and walked you into the first day of high school. How else would you have learned to love the smell of brownies, toasted bagels, onions and garlic sizzling in olive oil? Your body perfectly delivered the sounds of Stevie Wonder, Whitney Houston, and Bon Jovi right into your memories. She gave you your first kiss, which you felt on your lips and in your stomach, a coordinated body venture. She drove you to college and hiked the Grand Canyon. She might have carried your backpack through Europe and fed you croissants. She watched *Steel Magnolias* and knew right when to let the tears fall.

Maybe your body walked you down the aisle and kissed your person and made promises and threw flowers. Your body carried you into your first big interview and nailed it—calmed you down, smiled charmingly, delivered the right words. Sex? That is some of your body's best work. Your body might have incubated, nourished, and delivered a whole new human life, maybe even two or three. She is how you cherish the smell of those babies, the feel of their cheeks, the sound of them calling your name. How else are you going to taste deep-dish pizza and French onion soup? You have your body to thank for every good thing you have ever experienced. She has been so good to you.

And to others.

Your body delivered you to people who needed you the exact moment you showed up. She kissed away little tears and patched up skinned knees. She holds hands that need holding and hugs necks that need hugging. Your body nurtures minds and souls with her presence. With her lovely eyes, she looks deliberately at people who so deeply need to be seen. She nourishes folks with food, stirring and dicing and roasting and baking. Your body has sat quietly with sad, sick, and suffering friends. She has also wrapped gifts and sent cards and sung celebration songs to cheer people on. Her face has been a comfort. Her hands will be remembered fondly—how they looked, how they loved. Her specific smell will still be remembered in seventy years. Her voice is the sound of home.

You may hate her, but no one else does.

"It turns out that experiences of strength in our bodies, feeling the movement that we make in space, can influence the way we feel about our bodies," wrote McBride.

Our mind and body, together, are intricately interwoven, and together are all parts of who we are. This is why when we don't like our bodies, we feel badly about our whole selves. Or when we feel really powerful in our bodies, we feel really powerful in ourselves. If our identity is just as much our bodies as it is our minds and thoughts, then we can use our bodies to help us experience power in a way that is just as important to the self as having thoughts and ideas or words that make us feel powerful.[8]

This is called "embodiment" and essentially means you don't just hate or love your body as it *looks*, but you enjoy being in it. Can you imagine? It begins with mindfulness, this sense of paying attention to where your body is and what she is doing without being judgmental. While you are walking, stirring pasta sauce, soaking in the bathtub, carrying a baby, you are present and noticing what your body is accomplishing and experiencing. You are kind to her as she moves through the day's activities, thanking her for showing up and taking you places and finishing another day on this earth as good, good you.

In Dr. Niva Piran's "Developmental Theory of Embodiment," she explains three concepts that affect our ability to become mindfully embodied: mental freedom, social power, and physical power. We've unpacked the mental restrictions at length, including the myth we learn early that our bodies are objects to attract the male gaze while also being defective carriers needing constant reform. Another mental loop involves ways we are expected to act: engaging in "feminine" activities, acting demure, restraining appetites, and sexualizing relationships while competing with (or policing) other women. These norms become clear around middle school and sabotage our freedom to engage the world with agency, competence, power, and passion, liberties central to embodiment.

In short: when we are told that our bodies should look a certain way to attract men, that traits outside the standard should be bullied into submission, that girls should always be girly and muzzle our assertiveness, that sex and sexiness is our highest currency, and that other women are competitors, we have to work pretty damn hard to resist and reject those messages to attain mental freedom. Antidotes:

Practice shrewd media literacy: see it, notice it, name it, resist it.

Engage your interests whether they are "feminine" or not ("Hi, my name is Jen, and I hate malls and shopping but love football and barbecue.").

Stop aw-shucksing all the time.

Love what you love in big, hungry, blazing ways.

Don't use your body to appease, please, or manipulate men.

Treat other women like your sisters instead of rivals.

"But these have nothing to do with how I feel about my thighs," you may be saying. YES, THEY DO. These mental gremlins mutate when you feed them and turn our minds against our bodies. Don't underestimate the power of adjusting these dials toward body positivity. Western culture has handed us a truckload of outdated, oppressive conventions for women, and when we challenge them, a whole new world opens up to consider what makes each of us beautiful, how we want to live and move on this earth.

Dr. Piran also suggests that access to social power affects our ability to love our bodies. When we experience rejection or harassment for violating made-up rules about femininity, we often overcorrect to win the approval we lost (or never gained). We know the rules: we are promised acceptance and validation if we look and behave a certain way, so we play the game to get what is withheld from us by checking our real selves at the door and ceding power to self-appointed gatekeepers. We may not even know we do this; women are gifted at reading a room and giving it what it wants.

Social disempowerment can be as mild as being left out and as severe as victimization, and this is often tied to our appearance—physical attributes on one hand and race on the other. (Women of color experience double penalties as their race is also weaponized against them.) So if healthy embodiment is linked to increased social power, then the greater our privilege, the more positive our experience of "self." And the greater our dehumanization, the harder the fight to love our bodies. When we are loved, included, and respected, we feel better about our bodies, and vice versa. It all goes together. Do you see your own location on the sliding scale?

This one might feel impossible to battle since social standing is usually bestowed by other people, but we have a great deal of control over our own relational connections—and none of it involves manipulating our bodies to curry favor.

McBride suggests healthy embodiment here involves voice and intentional community. Environments that thrive on the social elevation of some and the disempowerment of others are not unchangeable; indeed, courageous voices from the margins have turned every oppressive power structure on its head. Voices calling out the bully, the mean girl, the misogynist, the boys' club, the manipulator, the passive aggressor, the racist, the intimidator, any person or group that uses social exclusion as capital—this critical resistance refuses to sail quietly along the constructed social tides that ebb and flow on human rejection.

Your voice matters. You are not powerless. You are not required to shape-shift for belonging; this is not a real rule and you don't have to follow it. "We can be tempted to satisfy our relational longings, our desire to connect, but in doing so deny the parts of us that make us who we really are," wrote McBride. "But the more we know ourselves, love ourselves, as we are, the more not being part of that group will feel like a manageable discomfort instead of social suicide."[9]

Raising our voices inside inequitable social environments will be their undoing, which is important work, but because healthy relationships are crucial to not just our mental health but the perception of our bodies, it is vital that we also choose individuals and groups who love us exactly as we are. I've learned a great deal on this from my friends of color who work in predominantly white environments. They spend so much energy code switching and assimilating and managing white culture and microaggressions, the only time their shoulders relax is with their family and friends of color, when their insides have permission to fully match their outsides and they are real, free, seen, cherished. Intentional community chosen for its sincere affection has no equal (more on this later). How long can we bang on the door of a house that doesn't want us? Antidotes:

Call out every instance of gender or sexual harassment: name it, report it, document it, fight it.

Call out exclusionary words, rules, or practices designed to keep some in and others out.

Speak up when *others* are excluded, shamed, harassed, or bullied.

Stop faking to fit in.

Choose relationships in which you are deeply loved as your entire real self.

Don't blame your body for the bad behavior of others.

When relationships are withheld or conditional, if we feel socially insecure, it deeply affects our experiences of ourselves, including our bodies. How many movies have we seen where the awkward "ugly duckling" girl is a social outcast until she gets a benevolent makeover, at which point the mean girls, in a shocking turn of events, now love her and want her at their table? A physical transformation is the genesis of every social reversal. This is not an invented storyline.

Whether we think critically about it or not, *we know* that social power is partially connected to appearance. Again, we've received that message since kindergarten. So if we are experiencing social disconnection, we automatically, if not subconsciously, blame our bodies. How we feel relationally correlates with how kind or hateful we feel toward our bodies. Inversely, healthy bonds with people who love us can erase some of this unidentified self-hatred. Could we take a hard look at the quality of our relationships? Would you consider this as a real factor affecting your body image? Maybe our thighs aren't the culprit after all.

Finally, Dr. Piran said a key factor in healthy embodiment includes physical power.[10] "Experiencing physical strength, or power, in our bodies" wrote McBride, "is surprisingly a really important element to loving ourselves and our bodies as they are."[11] We were most free in this space as girls. There was no delineation between where girls and boys played on the playground, who played soccer, who climbed trees, who rode bikes. Our bodies did what bodies wanted to do before gender conventions had any say. I was a quintessential tomboy—skinned knees, perched on limbs, climbing down gulleys, playing sports, which not all girls did, but they *could have*. At some point, we started hearing that physical power was not for pretty, desirable, or feminine girls. Or only a certain version of physicality was sanctioned. The message transitioned to: *sit like a lady; you throw like a girl; we don't play that; being tough is for boys; you don't want to bulk up; nobody likes an aggressive, competitive girl*. We lost the freedom of normal human body physical power.

Don't mistake this as a narrow factor only relatable to female athletes; physical strength looks a thousand ways with similar positive results. Example: my two besties, Jenny and Shonna, are wizards at "handyman" stuff. They can build bars and tables, hang shelves, paint two thousand square feet, build out closets. They measure and saw and nail gun and sew curtains. Their bodies do all that! Such strength! I am on record that if something terrible ever happens to Brandon, you'll find me hard-passing on Match. com and marrying these two. We will live happily ever after in a well-run, deeply organized house where I will cook and they will be my wives.

The link between physical power and body positivity is clear; I get this one. It feels good to be strong. It feels good to be physically powerful in any which way we can be; this is not just for women without disabilities (my friend Susie who uses a wheelchair is a member of a dance troupe called Body Shift that performs all over the city). If the other two theories of embodiment activate largely in our minds, this one lives in our muscles, bones, arms, and legs.

Not in an attempt to reduce them to a template but to appreciate the crazy awesome stuff our bodies can do. To be active in ways that bring us life, strong in ways that feel pretty kickass. There is nothing unfeminine about sweat or strength, sports or drive. This is what freedom in your body looks like, and it is good and wonderful.

"We're not stuck sitting with our legs crossed, hands clasped all day every day, but we can move our bodies in ways that we decided to move our bodies, and that we feel competent in our ability to do so. Lastly, physical freedom includes being comfortable with our physical desires, appetites, and changes that come with age. This means we don't beat ourselves up for feeling hungry, or how our skin or movements change with age, but embrace them as part of the story of our self and body in the world," wrote McBride.[12]

It's all just so kind, a completely different narrative than the one we learned. There is power in reintegrating our minds and bodies, caring for ourselves with compassion that understands we are not disembodied souls with unfortunate containers but whole people worthy of love, and oh so beautiful.

I adore what Elizabeth Gilbert wrote:

I've lost the dark (and particularly female) talent for self-criticism, and for tearing myself down. It feels like sacrilege. My mouth can't force the hateful words. And I can't bear it any-more, to hear another woman demean, degrade, or diminish herself. It shocks my senses and hurts my heart. To witness a woman denying that she is beautiful is like watching someone set fire to an art museum. It's like watching an angel drink gaso-line. It's like watching a Phoenix rip off its wings.[13]

I've been so mean to my body, outright hateful. I disparage her and call her names, I loathe parts of her and withhold care. I insist on physical standards she can never reach, for that is not how she is even made, but I detest her weakness for not pulling it off. I deny her things she loves depending on the current fad: bread, cheddar cheese, orange juice, baked potatoes. I push her too hard and refuse her enough rest. No matter what she accomplishes, I'm never happy with her. I've barely acknowledged her role in every precious experience of my life. I look at her with contempt.

And yet every morning, no matter how terrible I have been to her, she gets us out of bed, nurtures the family, meets the needs of the day. She tells me when I am hungry or tired and sends special red-alert signals when I am overwhelmed or scared. She has safely gotten me to and from a thousand cities with fresh energy. She flushes with red wine, which she loves, which is pretty cute. She walked the Cliffs of Moher in Ireland, the red dirt of Uganda, the steep opulence of Santorini, the ruins of Pompeii. She senses danger, trouble, land mines; she is never wrong. Every single time, she tells me when not to say something. She has cooked ten thousand meals. She prays without being told to; sometimes I realize she is whispering to God for us. She walks and cooks and lifts and hugs and types and drives and cleans and holds babies and rests and laughs and does everything in her power to live another meaningful, connected day on this earth.

She sure does love me and my life and family.

Maybe it is time to stop hating her and just love her back.

WHAT I NEED

4

I DESERVE GOODNESS

And now for a little story I've never talked about in full.

I wrote eight books before anybody read one. My kids were one, three, and five when I penned my first sentence sans contract in 2004, and they were ten, twelve, and fourteen before I officially made a living writing with Book Number Nine in 2012. Brandon was a student pastor, and, to help make ends meet, I watched other kids in my home, sold cherished possessions, hoarded spare change, and stole from Peter to pay Paul. Hot panic flooded my face whenever a cashier swiped my card; never was it *ever* guaranteed to go through. We barely kept the ship afloat, man.

All the while, I wrote and wrote, a naive recipient of dismal book contracts with no agent, no representation, turning in one unmarketed book a year (I never did a single interview for a single book), and pulling in around five thousand dollars annually from publishing. After eight years of committed work, I finally signed with an agent, wrote Book Number Nine with a decent contract, and it hit. *7: An Experimental Mutiny Against Excess* earned back its advance in the first quarter, and I received a royalty check for the first time. I was in the shower when Brandon burst in and slammed the check against the glass door so I could see it. I sat on the shower floor and sobbed.

7 was published by a conservative Baptist powerhouse, which was neither here nor there at the time. My agent shopped the book proposal around (so *that* is what agents do!), their offer came back the strongest, my rapport with the lead editor was fabulous, and they loved my concept. Having never experienced a genuine working relationship with a publisher before, as previously I'd basically turned in books and never heard from them again, I lacked the discernment to flesh this partnership out beyond the particulars of the contract. When publishers are trying to win a book, they speak as if you are a brilliant Christian Tina Fey who will change the landscape of literature. All that gushing is confusing, and you seize the opportunity before they remember you wrote eight books no one ever read.

7, against all odds and personal publishing history, delivered unexpected royalties every single quarterly cycle. It was the little engine that could, and it is no exaggeration to say it financially stabilized us and changed my career trajectory.

But then, when my husband and I made a public statement in 2016 embracing and affirming our LGBTQ brothers and sisters and friends and neighbors with no equivocation, I got a single text from my editor. There would be no discussion, and they asked no questions. They didn't just pull 7 off the shelves but they put it out of print. They had fifteen thousand copies in a warehouse, and we could pay for shipping or they'd destroy them. They pulled it off every retail site, Christian or not, and issued a press release denouncing me as their author and severing all ties. It was all done within twenty-four hours.

Not a single person from that publishing house, not one, ever called me, and I had worked closely with dozens of their staff. They didn't write me. They didn't explain their position or ask for clarity on mine. I received not a solitary kindness. Not a word. The punishment for having an inclusive theology for the LGBTQ community was swift.

It broke my heart, my family's heart. I had nightmares for months. It sent shockwaves through every person who loved me, partnered with me, or worked with me. It pulled a financial rug out from under our family. Several of this publisher's sanctioned authors wrote hit pieces online and piled on to the hysterical feeding frenzy. It was the loneliest I've ever felt, the most maligned, the most abandoned.

Even worse, to this day, several times a year that same publisher sends me a fancy box with someone's new book inside, packaged with colorful confetti, nestled next to some cute gift, and they ask me to promote it. I receive a hashtag to share, a tweet to cut and paste. The message crushes me: *I am unworthy of leadership but useful for free marketing. I cannot lead women to Jesus, but I can lead them to Amazon.*

I am recovered enough to finally say:

I did not deserve that.

I was a faithful leader and teacher for two decades, and I did not deserve that. I served with kindness, humility, and integrity, and I did not deserve that. My convictions were motivated by careful examination, serious inquiry, and sincere love, and I did not deserve that. I was a team player, a constant cheerleader, an enthusiastic contributor—*I was a good sister*—and that treatment was trash.

I deserved better.

It is a complicated matrix of factors that bar women from believing they deserve goodness. Inferiority complex, embarrassment, power differentials, fear, just for starters. Women are famous for putting up with crap. We take every manner of abuse and mistreatment, then employ mental gymnastics to make sense of it and somehow come out on the other side imagining we deserved it, we caused it, we should just take our licks and move on quietly. It hollows us out and sabotages our dignity, leaving us more vulnerable to debasement. This is a vicious cycle passed on for millennia. So let's start here:

You deserve goodness. Full stop.

Because you are a cherished human being created by a God who loves you. Because you bear the imprint of heaven. You are worthy of honor; every person is. You deserve the blessings of this earth-bound life like anyone else: to be deeply loved, to be wanted and seen, to be valued and treasured, to be productive and fruitful. You are not just a commodity for someone else's bottom line. You are not a utilitarian tool to be used and discarded. You are not dumb. You are not a problem. You are not inferior. You are not too much.

You didn't provoke someone else to abuse or harm or marginalize you in some way. You could not possibly be the *cause* of violence, injustice, exploitation; that is not how this works. Mistreatment doesn't begin with its target. It begins with the perpetrator, and how they choose to treat you is no reflection on what you do (or do not) deserve.

Unfortunately, though, while the last few generations have made remarkable strides toward equality in parts of the world, the primal impulse for women to expect less remains. It is pretty hardwired in us already but is further reinforced when we experience things like gaslighting, which has become, shockingly, somewhat of a social norm. What is gaslighting, you might be wondering? Gaslighting is a tactic in which a person or entity, in order to gain more power, makes a victim question their reality. Darlene Lancer, in an article for *Psychology Today* called it "a hidden form of mental and emotional abuse designed to plant seeds of self-doubt and alter your perception of reality."[1]

While gaslighting can be extreme, it can also be subtle:

I didn't say that. You misunderstood that. I have no idea what you're talking about. I can't believe you're doubting me like this. You are just too sensitive. That's not at all how it happened. This is your own insecurity making up a story. You know I would never hurt you. This was actually your fault. You caused this. All of us agree. We know how you are. No one else thinks that but you. The rest of us know the truth. I'm sure you think you understand, but you don't.

Someone benefits when you don't even believe you are worth good things, but a woman is unstoppable once she believes she deserves goodness.

So don't expect this one to go down without a fight.

Dr. Kristen Neff suggests *fierce self-compassion* as a starting place:

Compassion is aimed at the alleviation of suffering—that of others or ourselves—and can be ferocious as well as tender. These two poles are represented by the dialectic of yin and yang. Yin compassion is like a mother tenderly comforting her crying child. Yang compassion is like a mother bear ferociously protecting her cubs from harm. Traditional gender roles allow women to be yin, but if a woman is too yang—if she gets angry or fierce—people get scared and often insulting. Men are allowed to be yang, but if a man shows vulnerability he risks being kicked out of the boys' club of power. In many ways the #MeToo movement can be seen as the collective arising of female yang. We are finally speaking up to protect ourselves, our sisters, our daughters and sons.[2]

We understand the yin side of self-compassion, which looks like loving, self-connected comfort, validating our own pain in a nurturing manner. Taking gentle, mindful care of ourselves toward healing. This is more acceptable for women and less challenging, as it is subdued and largely internal. On the other hand, yang self-compassion looks like empowered truth, which fiercely protects us. It says *no* to harm and marginalization, refusing to accept anything less than goodness. We no longer avoid seeing or telling the truth in order to "keep the peace," which is, as Martin Luther King, Jr. wrote, a negative peace which is no peace at all.

"When we hold our pain with fierce empowered truth, we can speak up and tell our stories to protect ourselves and others from being harmed," wrote Dr. Neff, "but it is challenging to hold loving, connected presence together with fierce empowered truth because their energies feel so different." In other words, we tend to be inwardly tender or outwardly assertive, but not both. And yet the woman who believes she deserves goodness must exhibit each. We need love in our hearts so we don't become angry and hateful, but we need fierceness so harmful paths are disrupted.

Fierce self-compassion says unequivocally, "I deserve goodness, and so does everyone else."

In my best dreams, you are surrounded by men and women who believe this for you too. Who would never reap the benefits of your losses or keep you low so they can remain high. The best human people want goodness for all. It is a wondrous thing to belong to a charitable community committed to the highest good of its members. When you have a partner or spouse or friend group or church or work environment that cheers you on, celebrates your successes, pushes you toward new wins, cherishes your health— hang on with both hands and never let go.

To some degree, and we will explore this in depth in chapter

12, you choose to surround yourself with people who either believe you deserve goodness or don't. However, many of you are unpacking a childhood where you were harmed or poorly loved, and that is its own special work. We can't unpick our fathers, mothers, childhood experiences. When goodness was withheld from you at an early age, it requires monstrous energy as an adult to override. When children are blamed for the bad behavior of their parents or abused in any way, it creates an internal message board: *undeserving, unlovable, not worth the effort*. The world of possibility is shrunk, and goodness seems unreasonable.

"Your history can make you feel as if anything you perceive as positive about yourself couldn't be real. There's too much pain in your history to allow you to acknowledge your own unique specialness," wrote Dr. Suzanne Lachmann. She continued:

> The difficulty you have in trusting in yourself can make success or improvement seem even more remote. After all, if the way you were formed by your history and your consequent worldview contribute to feeling undeserving, then it can seem as if the improvements you make must be fleeting—as if they will inevitably be taken away or must be balanced by sliding backward in some other way. The process can be so insidious and subtle that you may not be able to articulate the experience. Still, the feeling of inevitable backsliding and unintentional self-sabotage is familiar for many of us.[3]

This looks a thousand ways.

You might blow up a good relationship because you'd rather burn them before they burn you, which you are positive they will.

You accidentally sabotage big days, happy moments, family celebrations, because the hope of goodness feels crushing. You are sure it will never deliver what you want it to or wish it had historically, so without even meaning to, you pick fights, over-control, criticize, and end up disappointed and weirdly ashamed.

Maybe the first setback toward your goal ends the whole game for you because, why even bother? You don't feel worth the effort. You knew you shouldn't have even tried.

Or you hide or justify horrible treatment because you feel unworthy of basic kindness; you may eventually pass that abuse on, your worst nightmare. You perpetuate what you endured.

Perhaps you are numb and empty—there is no expectation at all. You cannot even imagine a flourishing life full of joy.

I submit to you, dear ones, that the world of possibility is actually infinite, and goodness is your birthright and claim. Expect it. You do not need to ask permission or wonder if you are one of its recipients. In fact, you may insist upon it, which means you will not justify manipulation, bullying, condescension; disparagement, dismissal, belittlement; harassment, abuse, exploitation. You do not identify with your captor to spare his or her feelings. You recognize and resist self-sabotaging behaviors. You call shame what it is and refuse to submit to it. You certainly refuse to be defined by it, particularly if it originates from a fixed experience in your past. You show up for your life with bright eyes and clear expectations.

I was recently talking to a friend of mine who has a very public and visible life, and we were talking about managing public criticism (gawd). At one unforgettable moment, he recounted a life-changing moment with his therapist while discussing the surprising weight of public critique. She told him, "Okay, fine. If you are going to respond to negative comments online, if they get a big say in how you feel or create in the future, if you are giving them a front-row seat to your life, then I insist you also respond to every single positive comment to gauge the actual balance." And, of course, that would mean responding to one hundred lovely comments for every negative one, which would tip the scales correctly.

We are famously bad at assigning too much weight to criticism. Negative experiences retain an outsized influence on our mental health, because we cannot stay away from their destructive power, like moths to a flame. But if I spent proportional energy on positive and negative input, I would be forced to conclude that the world is mostly kind, generous, and connected . . . and a small bit of it is a dumpster fire.

"American society has spent a great deal of time and effort trying to promote people's self-esteem," Dr. M. R. Leary wrote in the *Journal of Personality and Social Psychology*, "when a far more important ingredient of well-being may be self-compassion. Rather than focusing on changing people's self-evaluations, *self-compassion changes people's relationship to their self-evaluations*. Self-compassion helps people not to add a layer of self-recrimination on top of whatever bad things happen to them."

In other words, life is hard enough; don't pile negativity on yourself while you are vulnerable. Stop kicking yourself when you are down and allowing negative input to reign while rejecting the good entirely. That is actually harder to come back from then the event itself.

Dr. Leary suggested three key aspects of self-compassion that we can learn to practice: self-kindness, common humanity, and mindful acceptance. In short:

Self-kindness means treating yourself tenderly, like you would someone you love, especially in suffering. You resist self-criticism and employ gentle care toward your own good soul. Be maternal. To yourself.

Common humanity involves you telling yourself, *I am not alone. Life is hard because it is hard, not because I am unworthy of goodness.* Don't take blame for what has been ubiquitous since the beginning of time.

Finally, *mindful acceptance* works to not overidentify with your own pain but to take a more detached observer's view. Don't attach additional meaning to it. Label it with no judgment,[4] and give yourself permission to move forward.

As a hypothetical example, if you are looking backward to a defining moment when you were deeply rejected by someone important, *self-kindness* might say, *That was so painful. I am not wrong to feel hurt. I can take the time to process that experience and grieve what should have been. I didn't deserve that. Common humanity* would say something like, *I am not alone. Some of the greatest people in history were rejected. I am not the first one to experience this exact type of pain. I have a huge pool of people to identify with and learn from. Mindful acceptance* could look like, *That person hurt me because they are a hurt person. It was unfair and unkind. It wounded me, and that will take a while to heal from, but this does not define me and I have permission to be happy again.*

We were created with divinity in our marrow. We are holy vessels meant for love and goodness. Everything about us was made for glory. I do not for a millisecond subscribe to the notion that God somehow profits off our losses or arranges great heartache as some showing of tough love. He has no hand in abuse, exploitation, or harm because he is incapable of evil. He is love and only love; there is no shadow side of Jesus.

Life breaks in so many ways because we live in failing bodies on a fluctuating earth with unchecked injustice where hurt people hurt people. Sometimes we reap what we sow, and sometimes we reap what someone else sows. Every generation has experienced unfathomable pain, because minds and bodies get sick and die, all of them. We lose and fail and suffer in every society, every culture, every subgroup, every family. We will be harmed and cause harm. This is the price of admission to being a human person with a life.

But I believe the original intent was nothing less than the garden of Eden and remains a possibility.

My dear friend Sarah Bessey rewires her spiritual circuitry by considering God as a mother, and if you believe we are made in the image of the divine like I do—"Let us make man in *our image . . . male and female* he created them"—then surely that does not only apply to the men created, and God is in fact both father and mother. Does it help debunk any notion of an arbitrary, punitive deity when we consider God taking on the role and characteristics of a mother? Would a good mother ever want anything other than goodness for her babies? Would she remain detached from their pain or judgmental of their struggles? She would delight in them simply because they exist, because they are hers. Her intentions would be only good.

This adoration applies to all of us, which is hard to accept. How can people deserve goodness when they are the actual worst? What of the abusers and charlatans? I cannot pretend to know how God loves us all, because I sure don't, but I suspect that centuries of injustice and evil and fear wreaked so much havoc on the heart of mankind and caused such damage generation to generation that all we can see from our low vantage point are the effects. But from a high, divine view, even people who cause great harm have something precious at their core, something worth loving, something that might have been deeply good had it not been so ruined.

I think often of the most heinous evildoers at age six. Who was hurting them, deceiving them, breaking them back then? Is any baby born deserving anything less than goodness? God would say no—particularly if we consider the mother perspective. Somehow God can love us even after life corrupts us, and there is always a path home to the goodness we were born for.

This matters for more than our own health, because goodness begets goodness. We pass on what we value. This feels impossible, but Brandon and I have parents married almost fifty years each. Our parents love each other so deeply, it is almost embarrassing.

Get a room, you guys! We've watched our parents serve and persist and laugh and hang on and practice devotion all these years. Their love poured out on everyone around them, and it mattered. Our family has a mostly healthy uplink, which pays forward. This is what my kids think life is: parents and grandparents and aunts and uncles invested in one anothers' goodness and theirs.

Of course, we get on our kids' nerves, and our parents get on ours. Of course, we fight. (I am notoriously tender in conflict, and my siblings recall with great delight a road trip in our VW van when mom and dad were fighting in the front seat—super rare because my dad burned hot and my mom was the baking soda—and my sibs carried on with their coloring books while I bawled hysterically like a newborn baby because I just knew their marriage was doomed. I was a real snowflake.) We've also had some terrible sorrow in our family, too private to discuss, so I am no Pollyanna, trust me. But goodness mostly begets goodness, and we send out what we believe internally. If our insides are filled with shame and self-disgust, we operate out of that poison with everyone else. If we don't believe we deserve goodness, it is hard to believe anyone else does either. We distribute soul health, or we distribute shame.

We fight for this in our own lives, so we can fight for it in everyone else's. We believe it for ourselves, so we can believe it for others. Grab hold of this truth, so you can look someone else in the eye and assure them they are worthy of good things, no matter what they've been told. Folks full of goodness are the ones we need. They are our best teachers, our kindest leaders, our healthiest parents, our most generous friends. Do this work, so you can pour it back out on the people you love and live by, serve and cherish. Fierce self-compassion pays its greatest dividends in the way we are able to love. Insist that you are worth the work, because the people you adore are worth your best.

We don't just look backward to reclaim goodness but forward

to claim what does not yet exist. You deserve good things still! You have a lot of pavement left. Maybe this is the moment in your life you finally believe it. You can't relive the days behind you, but you sure can reimagine the days to come. It is never too late. I am forty-five and in full possession of this knowledge: this is all we get and it is going fast. One life, one body, one family, one shot. My patron saint Anne Lamott put it like this:

> What if you wake up some day, and you're 65, or 75, and you never got your memoir or novel written; or you didn't go swimming in warm pools and oceans all those years because your thighs were jiggly and you had a nice big comfortable tummy; or you were just so strung out on perfectionism and people-pleasing that you forgot to have a big juicy creative life of imagination and radical silliness and staring off into space like when you were a kid? It's going to break your heart. Don't let this happen.[5]

This ridiculous world is chock-full of goodness! It is everywhere. It is yours. It was always meant for your pleasure and participation. No one else is more or less deserving of living this delicious life with gusto. What does goodness look like to you? Is it healthy relationships full of connection and joy? Exciting dreams where you put your hand to the plow and do what you were made for? Freedom to be who you are as you are? Liberation from a toxic person or place? Slowing down? Amping up? You are the person to claim it. No one is going to do this for you, especially if they are dependent on the status quo you help maintain. This is your work, yours to say *I deserve this wonderful thing, and I don't deserve this lesser thing.* Goodness abounds; it just needs your compliance.

Even if you've royally screwed up your life, your family, your career. Even if you only experienced harm and have no precedence for good things. Even if you are the difficult person in the equation. Even if you did the worst thing, the thing you hate most. Even if no one in your world believes it. Even if everyone in your world believes it but you. Like I said, there is always a path home to the goodness we were born for. Maybe it starts with some hard work:

> Drawing boundaries, speaking up, creating safety.
> Asking forgiveness, making amends, taking responsibility.
> Prioritizing recovery, healing, soul care.
> Working on sobriety, mental health, addiction.
> Saying, "I'm sorry," "I hurt you," "I want more for us."
> Saying, "I hear you," "I forgive you," "I'm still here."
> Saying, "I forgive you from afar but will never reengage for
>   my future."
> Drawing near to God in that way children do to their
>   mothers . . . or coming back after having been away.
> Naming big dreams, new goals, hidden hopes.
> Closing the door gently on what is behind and throwing it
>   open for what is ahead.

Goodness must be fought for. It doesn't come easily in this harsh world that insists we prioritize cynicism, anger, fear, shame. Fury is better currency, frankly. Despair or inertia bob along the waters without any help. Our cultural equilibrium will not naturally settle on The Deserved Goodness of Humanity. It has too many enemies conspiring to unbalance the equation: power, patriarchy, fear, regret. If you still struggle to imagine it for yourself, could you imagine it for your children, your beloved people? Is it so hard to envision a world in which they deserve good things and not harm?

This work begins in our minds, transfers to our expectations, materializes through our words, and emerges through our actions.

You know when you see a woman who has done this work. She is full of joy and generosity; she loves herself well, which seems rare these days. She is hung up on exactly none of the garbage the rest of us are. She laughs and loves demonstratively. You never catch her absolving small behavior but calling people to live big, love big, dream big, forgive big. You know her dreams because she is chasing them; she feels worthy of their importance. She employs healthy boundaries with people who prefer her subservience, and their disapproval doesn't define her. This alone feels miraculous, yes? She is absolutely certain, and you could not convince her otherwise, that *everyone* deserves goodness, and you won't catch a whiff of jealousy, schadenfreude, or superiority. She knows she is loved, so she knows everyone is loved, even when they don't know it and act out of brokenness.

You know her, because at some point in your life, she has probably loved you well.

I am determined to be this woman. Join me.

5

I NEED SOME HELP

A few years ago, Brandon and I, along with four other best friends, took a dreamy, over-the-top trip to Spain, Italy, Croatia, and France. We were loud, demonstrative Texans ready to experience the Renaissance civilization. In our preplanning research, we noted that Naples was rather infamous for pick-pocketing and low-level crime, and let it be said: we were prime targets. We deserved to be looted. I would want to rob us if I were Neapolitan.

Going through Naples, we had to use their trolley system to find the train to Pompeii. We found the trolley but couldn't tell which one to get on and which train to get to, and we were basically big dumb-dumbs huddled around an iPhone app, pointing in different directions and taking up too much space. I know you can envision this and I know you hate us, and I accept that as fair. At this point, an older man standing nearby, probably in his seventies, noticed our Americanness and offered to help us. We told him where we were going, and he cheerfully grabbed us by the hands and ushered us onto a trolley, volunteering to take us personally all the way there.

On the trolley, we continued in our Texan way to talk too loudly about where we were going, which involved the route our Italian Benefactor had explained. As we discussed and our IB nodded, several people around him cut their eyes at us and shook their heads ever so imperceptibly. One of them mouthed aggressively, "NO." Danger, Will Robinson!

Unsure if these Italians were simply warning us off a slightly slower route or something north of that like adult kidnapping, we closed ranks and whispered furiously about our impending future. Were we going to lose twenty-five minutes on a more circuitous trolley path than necessary? Or were we about to be victimized by a mastermind robbery ring executed by elderly Italian grandfathers? We couldn't know. Sure, there were six of us weighing a combined one-and-a-half tons, but we suddenly felt terrified of this senior citizen who—I could not possibly make this up—was helping an even older gentleman onto the trolley while wrapping his scarf gently around his neck, all as we debated whether or not he was aiming to rob, traffic, or murder us.

Our iPhone app suggested an alternative path to the one our escort charted, and when we approached the stop, we grabbed our bags and rushed onto the platform like hostages escaping a bunker. Distraught, he reached for us as we fled and, in the most devastated tone as the doors were closing, cried: "Why you no trust me??"

Having barely escaped with our lives, we took the next trolley to a different stop, then another, then another, until we finally made the train station. Upon entering, we studied the master map to determine how close we'd been to abduction, and, lo and behold, had we stayed his course, we would have been there twenty minutes and two stops sooner. We had broken an old man's heart who was just trying to be kind.

Why you no trust me?

WE ARE MONSTERS.

I submit that most of us are pretty bad at help. Bad at asking for it, then weirdly bad at accepting it. This ranges from isolated moments of unnecessary self-reliance to being absolutely lost at sea before raising the flag, at which point we are so far from the shore no one can even see us drowning. This can compromise any number of relationships and environments: our marriages and homes, our careers and workplaces, our friendships and communities, our mentorships and churches. To say nothing of the crushing weight of bearing burdens alone without the warm hand of human kindness to push us through or even push us up, helping us reach for dreams and goals and new spaces.

Like everything else, this has tendrils that reach pretty far back in our experiences. We learned early how our families felt about help. What kind of signals did you receive on asking for help as a kid? Did your family place a high value on doing it yourself, or did they model what it looks like to let other folks contribute? When you did ask for help, how did the people in your life respond?

"If the messages you got, overtly or covertly, taught you that reaching out was unacceptable, futile, or would cause more pain, it makes sense that you would go it alone whenever possible," wrote psychotherapist Lisa Ferentz. "Your past experiences with family, teachers, peers, and other significant people in your life served to either reinforce the notion that help was available, consistent, predictable and safe, or left you with the painful impression that your needs would go unheard and unanswered."[1]

It is a tricky scorecard to read, because sometimes facing appropriate moments of forced independence as a kid feels scary (who wants to grow up and do stuff on their own if they don't have to?), but those experiences typically shake out from an entire childhood of "You're on your own, camper." When my seventh grader Remy brings me her math homework after looking at it for a whopping ten seconds, this is how it goes:

Me: Oh, that's not my work. That's yours.

Remy: But you're my mom. You are supposed to help me.

Me: I already completed seventh grade. I passed in 1986. I have receipts.

Remy: My teacher didn't teach this.

Me: You are telling me your teacher didn't give one word of math instruction and just sent thirty thirteen-year-olds home to guess? Wow. I'd better email her and find out why she isn't teaching her classes anymore. She should probably get fired! What is her name again?

Remy: FINE. I'LL TRY.

This is not the sort of adolescent tomfoolery I am talking about. We all have had moments of utter laziness disguised as helplessness, and if our parents weren't too precious, they sent us packing. But there is a difference between the normal reluctant march toward independence and a childhood culture of mandatory self-reliance. If you experienced the latter, asking for help might feel impossibly vulnerable, an opportunity for rejection you engineered yourself.

Then come the social barriers characteristic of adulthood in Protestant work-ethic America, chief of which is not wanting to appear needy or weak. Where we ever got the idea that asking for help signals incompetence, I have no clue. As clinical social worker Louis Laves-Webb wrote,

Given the strong western societal emphasis on individualism and self-reliance, asking for help can initially appear culturally counter to some of the "value-propositions" of what it means to be an American. However, upon deeper examination, *the failure to ask for help when needed tends to perpetuate self-neglect much more than self-reliance.* No one person can do it all by themselves. Societies function within a system, neighborhoods function within a system, and families function within a system. When we fail to ask for help when needed, we simply fail to utilize the systemic support surrounding us.[2]

In other words, we do not become stronger but weaker when we refuse to say, "I need some help."

This area is perhaps where women are the least sincere and suffer the most in silence, conditioned as we are to project competency while minimizing struggle. *We're awesome! We got this! We can handle everything like our moms and grandmas did! All these damn kids are going to rise up and call us blessed!*

Allow me to say this first: you should acknowledge all the shiz you get done. Women spin the plates, pay the bills, sign the forms, do the work, fix the problems, manage the people, organize the world. If you made a list of everything you execute in a calendar week and put someone else's name at the top of the page, you would give her an A+. You would name her as your patroness. You would cover her with an afghan and make her a cuppa tea.

You are, in fact, an incredibly competent badass.

I don't know a woman who is not holding her world together. As someone who primarily serves women, I stand in regular awe of our community. The things we are dreaming, imagining, accomplishing, enduring—why aren't we in charge of everything? Our capacity for hard work is unmatched. We are excellent at adulting, even though we say we aren't. If we helicoptered out of our lives, one thousand things would unravel.

You have the right to be proud of all you do. That is a healthy assessment of your own life. Ironically, however, it is unhealthy pride that sometimes keeps us from asking for help, even if that pride shape-shifts as shame.

When my kids were babies and toddlers, Brandon worked seventy hours and five nights a week, as he was required to ("Work for the church!" they said. "It will be so great!" they said. GTHO). I have virtually no memories of him from that time period. I had three kids in diapers and pull-ups and preschool, and I stayed home with them because 1) I begged to, and 2) with my teacher salary, I would have taken home $17.54 a week after childcare costs for three.

Listen up, young mamas. I have now parented through all the stages, including college, and nothing, absolutely nothing, compares to the exhaustion of early childhood. I have never worked so hard in my living life. Parenting littles is a complete crush of fatigue, hilarity, boredom, and delirium. Running the gauntlet of elementary school requirements for twenty straight years is less hard. Parenting fifty middle schoolers would be less hard. Riding with horrid teenage drivers where you almost die once a minute is less hard. The president of the United States does less work. The littles, man. Stay-at-home parenting, man. I can't believe I recovered any brain functionality. You just *survive* early childhood.

But I asked for it, and I wanted to be awesome. (Note: I *was* awesome. Same as you.) I'm actually really proud of those years; I just wasn't prepared for how hard it would be, how draining, how lonely. I was operating in the red with no idea how to pull the account back to black. But hell if I was going to admit it to Brandon, who I was somehow mad at for not reading my mind. I refused to ask for his help while also being furious he didn't notice I needed it. I wanted to slay at this with no cracks in the armor while also wishing he would see all the cracks. Didn't they teach mind-reading at Man School?

However, one super hard, frustrating day, tucked away in our upstairs bedroom, I finally broke to my mom on the phone and poured my guts out, lamenting the exhaustion of parenting all those freaking kids mainly solo. I mean, tears-pouring-down-my-face belly sobs. It all rushed out: the loneliness, the resentment, the weariness. As a certifiable type-A achiever not prone to admitting anything resembling need, this was weird territory for me. And apparently for Brandon, too, who stood in the doorway with his jaw hanging open, God bless and keep him.

This was news to him. Crying to my mom? He has seen me do that maybe one time since. Hiding my depletion and tattling to my mother was perhaps the worst possible way to handle my limitations. I'll never forget how shocked he was, how hurt that I had routed around him, how surprised he was at the cracks. Fun fact: when you pretend like you are perfectly managing everything, people believe you!

As it turned out, Brandon and I were in this parenting thing together, and plenty of simple solutions existed to distribute the load a bit. Brandon started staying home on Fridays until noon, and, looky here, I was out the door by 7:00 a.m. like it was my job. Those five unregulated hours a week, in addition to a few other easy levers we pulled, turned me into a new human. The kids had Daddy Fridays, which meant, well, I don't actually know or care. I was at brunch. Bye, Felicias.

How can you do the same and start being more honest about needing help? Ferentz recommends starting with these questions:

What are the situations in your life that would benefit from outside help and support?

Who are the people in your life who would be safe to reach out to for assistance?

What resources would you encourage a best friend to use if they needed help?

In the quiet of your interior self, is there a role or task where you feel either overwhelmed or unequipped? It could be that your account is overdrawn, and you need help to restore it to abundance. No one can do everything. Don't be arrogant.

Or maybe you are considering new territory and need mentorship, advice, instruction. Being a learner is underrated. The best people I know are constantly learning, putting themselves humbly under the leadership of others who've gone before them. This is no indicator of weakness but rather healthy ambition. That woman is unafraid of a challenge and cares enough about her own development to ask for help and secure the outcome she wants. Learners become our most effective leaders.

The *Harvard Business Review,* in a study of design firm IDEO's exceptional culture of collaboration, discovered several principles about this very thing that apply not only to other work environments but really to life in general.

Not every large company's leader would, if asked about organizational priorities, bring up the topic of encouraging collaborative help in the ranks. But IDEO's leadership is explicitly focused on it. For Tim Brown, the CEO, that's not only because the problems IDEO is asked to solve require extreme creativity; it's also because they have become more complicated. Brown said, "I believe that the more complex the problem, the more help you need. And that's the kind of stuff we're getting asked to tackle, so we need to figure out how to have a culture where help is much, much more embedded." Essentially, this is a conviction that *many minds make bright work.*[3]

I'd love for us to pick up that nugget of wisdom before moving on: the more complex the problem, the more help we need. I feel that rub against some internal set of personal expectations I carry, because I sometimes think solving complex issues solo demonstrates acumen. The harder the task, the more impressive I am for executing it. The bigger the stakes, the bigger the glory or some such nonsense. When, in fact, a collaborative culture produces better results every time. Learning to ask for help is not just good for altruistic reasons; it makes practical sense and increases productivity. Many minds make bright work indeed.

Consider the following two paths in your area of need—family, work, health, relationship repair, new goals, whatever. In the first, you set this collaborative intention on the front end. You believe that the combined effect of group work or group discussion is greater than the sum of its parts. You prioritize results over personal credit. You evaluate the role or task or issue in front of you and decide to honor collaboration, to encourage it, model it, use it, put it in place as the standard operating procedure. Then, you drop the need in the middle. *Here is the goal; let's accomplish this together.*

Or, you decide to be impressive, independent, disassociated. You won't ask for input or help, either out of pride ("I'll conquer this myself") or reluctance ("No one has time to help me"). You plan to meet your need to the best of your abilities, as far as they will take you. You jump in with good intentions but hit the natural end to your limits, not because you are a weakling but because you are human like everyone. You have twenty-four hours in a day and only know what you know. You are in the weeds. Overwhelmed, your stress comes out sideways in resentment, passive aggression, anger, or despair. Or you simply hit the ceiling, and there is nowhere else to go. You have the capacity for more, the ability for success, but it requires new input, other minds to make your work brighter.

We invent objections to asking for help, claiming it would be too much of an inconvenience for others, that people aren't inclined to help, but research tells us a different story. In the two-year examination of IDEO's helping culture, researchers wrote, "In the office we studied, nearly every person was named as a helper by at least one other person. Even more amazing, an overwhelming majority of employees (about 89%) showed up on at least one other employee's list of top five helpers. Clearly, effective helping isn't a rare skill."

People want to help! Loads of behavioral science confirms that communities who serve one another, borrow from one another's skills, and strengthen group potency are healthier and happier. "Surveying *both givers and receivers of help*, we found that the experience of successful helping boosted morale and job satisfaction."

People like helping, because it is good for them too.

I am the lucky member of a small friend tribe of authors, influencers, and public servants. There are six of us, and we have been like sisters for almost a decade. There is a great deal of crossover to our work, and we speak career shorthand in a way like-minded women can. From three different countries, we are intertwined in one anothers' lives nearly every day of the year through Voxer (what a time to be alive!), but we set aside four days at the beginning of each January to spend together in person come hell or high water.

At least one of the days looks like this: with our laptops open, we focus on one woman at a time and discuss every aspect of her life and career.

What dilemma do you have right now? What is coming up? Where is something not working? What does your family need right now? What is your next goal? Where do you want to be in five years? Where do you need help? What have you learned? What dials can you turn? Who do you need to hire? How is your team functioning? Can we work through your content together? What needs to go?

According to the rules of the world, we should be independent competitors reluctant to share our slices of the pie, but we take the exact opposite approach. These women are among the greatest loves of my life. Anything good I've pulled off in the last few years has been incubated with these five first. We've sorted through every single family issue; created our own personal parenting mastermind group; reorganized one anothers' books; shared assistants; edited first, middle, and final drafts; contributed research; written for one anothers' spaces; promoted each person's work like it was our own; and written marketing plans for every project (okay, fine, that is mainly Sarah Bessey; underneath her happy-clappy, tea-drinking, sweater-knitting Jesus exterior beats the heart of a world-class marketer). In fact, Kristen Howerton and I just found out our books come out the same month, and my first reaction was, "SISTER BOOKS!"

Would you consider that the folks you admire most, the ones thriving in the career you want or living in a vibrant way that makes your heart swell are there because they asked for a lot of help along the way? And do still? They are not too proud to ask for assistance, admit when they are stumped, learn from other people, reinforce their weaknesses. Nor do they hesitate to share credit, pass the microphone, celebrate the victories of others, consider it a group win.

There is no such thing as a self-made woman. Oh sure, there are those who *act* like they are, but peel back the curtain and you will discover help upon help upon help. I am not interested when greatly assisted people flaunt their successes, then suggest everyone else could achieve the same if they tried harder. It infuriates me when successful women pretend they got there on nothing but grit. Hogwash. Let's all stop pretending, swallow our counterproductive pride, and learn how to ask for help.

Professor Wayne Baker at the University of Michigan proposed five ways to get better at asking for help.[4] I've listed them below and added my own commentary.

1. *"Earn responses to your requests by generously helping others in the first place."* Those who help others are among the first helped when they need it. If you build relational capital by consistently

jumping in when people need you, you create a give-and-take community that makes for the brightest work. In fact, "The desire to repay help appears to be hard-wired in the human species . . . and the norm of reciprocity is so powerful that you can generally expect help if you've helped others. This also yields a psychological benefit for those wary of reaching out— it's much easier to reconcile asking for help when you yourself have been helpful."

Don't miss that hidden benefit. Some deeply wired part of us is reluctant to ask for help when we rarely give it ourselves. We have a debtor's mentality and think, *Now I owe them.* But, when helping is a natural part of your life, you inoculate yourself from some of that aversion. This is maybe God's way of keeping us from being assholes. This is how you build a community or culture of reciprocity. It grows layer by layer until you have a well-connected group of helpers who are sincerely glad to do so. Stephen Covey calls this "sowing good will," and there are worse things to cultivate.

2. *"Know what you want to ask for."* Sometimes we have a sense of the issue at large but haven't thought through exactly what we need to address it. *Just help me more at home! I can't do this work project alone! I can't manage this team by myself! I am drowning in the needs of my kid!* The danger in stalling is that situations can grow from a problem into a crisis, at which point you are likely hysterical and your potential helpers are clueless. This step is as simple as focusing on the problem at hand, writing down your goals, and then listing action steps and resources needed to accomplish each. (Author's note: I often need a helper to sort this part out. Impartial, strategic thinkers can sometimes see a clear path through what only feels muddy to us. A helping helper to help us think through who can help us and how. Tip your waitress, folks.) Rather than let it all exist in

some nebulous world called *Effing Overwhelmed*, give it careful attention and think through your ask.

Wherever you feel overwhelmed or underresourced—this is where you need help. What are your goals? Not just how you feel now, but where do you want to go? What is your desired endgame? More order and less chaos? Fewer moving parts? A career change? A more reciprocal marriage? Children who contribute and take responsibility? A successful work project? Education toward a pressing need? Mentorship toward a pressing ambition? Stronger engagement from your team or volunteers? Support in your work toward mental or emotional health? Recovery partners?

With your endgame in hand, thoughtfully consider what you need to get there. Who do you know with expertise or experience in this area? Who is your natural partner in this? What resources would be invaluable? What environment would be your best classroom? What very specific request can you make? What will actually help you? Specially, pointedly, intentionally. Firm up your ask, and then you are ready to make it.

3. *"Ask SMARTly."* Many requests are so poorly worded, it's difficult to respond. So rather than ask in a way that confuses people, let's learn to ask in a way that makes it easier for them:

S: SPECIFIC. This is where Step Two plays in. You are not throwing an ambiguous problem against the wall and expecting someone to intuitively know how to help you. You've thought it through and have a clear ask. *This is what I need, and this is exactly how you can help me.*

M: MEANINGFUL. Why do you need this? Embed your request in the context of your humanity. This is how you are overwhelmed, why you have reached your limits, or where you dream of going. Rather than blaming your helper for not showing up sooner or better, this is about you.

A: ACTION-ORIENTED. Ask for something to be done. This is the specific ask taken one step further. A generic "Can you help me?" followed by a "Sure" can equal nothing real quick. Most helpers are grateful for this specificity. This is the most direct line from your need to the solution.

R: REAL. Your need should be authentic, not made up. Folks who ask for help in consistently hyperbolic situations, or inside crises they create, or as an attention grab can only cry wolf so many times. That is a toxic cycle that will burn out every helper in a hundred-mile radius.

T: TIME-BOUND. When do you need this by? Again, eliminate every vague factor and make helping you crystal clear. If this feels too forward, the research shows that folks absolutely prefer clarity and deadlines. You are making this easier for them, not harder.

4. *"Don't assume you know who and what people know."* Under-estimating what others can and will do to help is a common mistake. Truthfully, you don't know the extent of what anyone knows or how they can help until you ask them. When you aren't sure where to turn (as opposed to some scenarios when you know exactly who to ask), a specific request delivered to a pool of potential helpers can yield extraordinary results.

Does anyone have a contact at _____ and can you connect us via email?

Does anyone have any experience with _____ and would you have ten minutes for a phone call?

My child has been diagnosed with _____ and I am looking for another mom in this community.

My team has hit this roadblock _____ and I am looking for an advisor to spend an hour coaching us through it.

Help lurks in unexpected places all the time. Last month during my Sunday sermon, I talked about a recent trip to the Mexico border to learn about the immigration system and how to serve separated families. Having only returned two days before that Sunday, I mentioned that my head was swimming with information and I was still unable to sift through it for any cohesive next steps. A tall gentleman, new to our little church, approached me after the service, and he said, "I am an information strategist. This is literally what I do. Here is my card. I'd be glad to sit down with you and wrangle all this complicated data into something manageable so you lead forward." Boom. I could've never known to ask him, because I didn't even know him. But because I put the need out into the sanctuary, my helper stepped forward.

5. *"Create a culture where asking for help is encouraged."* Make it easy to ask for and give help by setting the tone, norms, and practices in your environment. Coach your colleagues and friends and children from the get-go to *expect* to need help, ask for it, and give it; then make it a regular practice you yourself model. Rather than reinforcing impossible standards of self-reliance, write a new story for your little world.

One last note: sometimes the help we need is clinical. If you are drowning in a sea your regular people are not equipped to swim in, if what you need is deeply rooted and requires the care of a professional, nothing is more courageous than saying this out loud and moving toward your own healing. As I mentioned earlier, the failure to ask for help when needed tends to perpetuate self-neglect much more than self-reliance. I cannot say this any plainer: there is no shame in securing counseling, therapy, medication if appropriate, and soul care. Rather, it is the strongest possible response to your own pain. Miles Adcox of Onsite said, "Therapy is not an indicator of what is wrong with you but what is right with you. In fact, therapy is a gift people don't *need* but *deserve*."[5]

Healthy, integrated women speak up when they need help. What they feel on the inside, they say on the outside. They choose not to bury their needs out of fear or pride, because those get buried alive. You better believe those needs will rise from the dead. They'll come out of our mouths stinging with passive aggression, out of our body language seething with resentment, out of our eyes in tears of frustration, out of our posture sagging under unrealized dreams. We're fooling no one, not even ourselves.

Let's deal with our lives! Let's face our issues head on and make good use of the community of people who love us, work with us, live with us. We are grown-ups mature enough to be humble learners, honest truth tellers, collaborative cheer-leaders, askers and givers of help. I want to be the generation that rejects the poisonous idea of self-reliance, refuses to pass it on to our kids, and instead creates beautiful communities full of generosity. What a wonderful story to live! What a beautiful story to write! And I firmly believe that a rising tide lifts every boat in this harbor. People thrive in helping cultures, bottom lines increase, productivity expands, dreams materialize, fear recedes, pride is shared rather than hoarded, and souls awaken, because love is the currency. This is the better way to live.

Many minds make bright work, and we have tons of good work to do.

6

I NEED MORE CONNECTION

My two best girlfriends and I live within forty-five seconds of each other. Jenny, Shonna, and I have around twenty million shared memories. As I type this paragraph, we are at the lake together, and I am upstairs writing while they are downstairs painting the walls after organizing my closets. (We made a sunset happy-hour date for 5:30 on the deck, because I always feel like I need a prize for doing my job. *Where is my gold star for doing the normal work I am paid to do?* asks the Enneagram Three.)

We have traveled the world together on points and miles and rewards, employing a very, very tacky tradition: in every place we visit, we buy matching sweatshirts with that city's name on it. Good People of Style, I do not mean trendy sweatshirts that look cute over leggings or paired with skinny jeans. We hunt for the ugliest, most ill-fitting, obnoxious sweatshirts we can find. We prefer to buy them in a gas station or from a sketchy street vendor. They must absolutely scream "tourists." We like to get them three sizes too big since they will shrink in half upon washing like $5.99 sweat-shirts do. Although not required, it delights us if either the font or the entire thing is somewhere between loud and fluorescent. We will not purchase if there is not one for each of us, for they must be matching or what is even the point of traveling?

Then, and this part is crucial, we wear them while still in that city. All three of us. Our husbands love this, except the opposite of that. (Our crown jewel was getting our names screen-printed in Greek while in Athens, which we then wore on our bike tour.) We do this unironically and with no shame. The rule is: we shall not explain ourselves. No side wink to our waiter. No "we're just being silly" comments to our guide. No explanation of our match-ing XXL coral sweatshirts that say "I ♥ SF" while at dinner in the Bay Area. We stand by our fashion choices with great dignity, like three gaudy Queen Elizabeths.

Our friend Amy traveled with us to Seattle once, and months later, while organizing our church's garage sale, Jenny found the matching fire-engine red sweatshirt we'd forced her to purchase in one of the boxes, marched over to her with the orphaned souvenir in hand, and, in a low, terrifying voice, said:

"Explain. Your. Self."

The sweatshirts are forever. I don't know why I even have to explain this. They are a package deal with this sisterhood forged through a thousand fires, a million conversations, and a billion shared laughs. I credit my girlfriends for the deep sense of belong-ing that has sustained me through an unexpected public life. Although hyperbole is my medium, with absolutely no exaggera-tion, I cannot imagine my life without them. I have no vision for it; no imaginable existence.

A connected life drunk with rich relationships is central to my soul theology. I hold many elements of my life loosely. My career and platform matter enormously, and I aim to offer the truest, best work I am capable of, but if it went away or shifted, I'd adjust my sails. However, if all I was left holding were relationships with my family and closest community, if that is all that remained, I would still consider myself the luckiest girl on earth. My life derives its greatest meaning, its power and energy, from the people I love who love me too.

I was on the phone once with a fellow Christian leader whom I've led beside for years, if only in ancillary circles. She and I operate out of different theologies with wildly different styles, but a sister is a sister, right? As we discussed our disparate approaches, I told her, "In Jesus' awesome summary of life's main work—love God and love people—you lean into the 'love God' part best and I lean into the 'love people' part best. We both do both obviously, but we are naturally geared toward one."

Loving people just makes sense to me. I am unable to separate policy, theology, rhetoric, theories, or interpretations from the people they affect. I lack all objectivity. I evaluate the merit of every idea based on how it bears upon actual people. It matters to me that folks know they are beloved and have every opportunity to belong and thrive in their communities. And, to be clear, I believe loving people fits perfectly under the umbrella of loving God, so when "loving God" results in pain, exclusion, harm, or trauma to people, then we are absolutely doing the first part wrong. It is not God in error but us.

Loving people is a must, because close personal relationships are not just desirable but *essential* for well-being. How do I know this? Again, since I believe we were created with great purpose, including built-in biological rewards for connected behavior, it makes perfect sense that science explains the benefits of relationships on our minds and coping abilities and general health. God and science could not possibly contradict (again, if we think they do, it is our error, not God's), so I'm always eager to learn from biologists and sociologists and psychologists about connectedness and, by extension, why it's important to love people. Through their work, I see how God designed us to flourish. I see why he told us to live deeply in community, including explicit detail on the practices required for the long haul: forgiveness, humility, service, compassion. Inversely, I understand that any "obedience to God" that results in dehumanization could not possibly be holy. I don't tell my kids not to hit, then outfit them with boxing gloves.

So here is what science tells us about relationships. The leading theory in psychological well-being, called Self-Determination Theory (SDT), names three pillars of emotional health: autonomy (being in control of your own life), competence (being capable to succeed and thrive), and relatedness (being in close personal relationships). SDT founders posit that, to the extent these three needs are met, people will experience wellness, but to the extent they are unmet, people will suffer.[1]

The interesting thing is, that third need, relatedness, is not the only need satisfied in high-quality relationships, which you might think, but the autonomy need and, to a lesser degree, the competence need are also met because our best people support those two qualities in us. That is how powerful connectedness is; it alone has the capacity to meet virtually every need we have to flourish as humans. When we have meaningful relationships with people who say, "I believe in you, and you can do this," we start on third base instead of in the batter's box.

In a study published in the *Personality and Social Psychological Review*, professors Brooke Feeney and Nancy Collins studied how positive relationships promote or hinder "thriving" and found two key effects.[2] One is enabling us to chase purpose and meaning. In other words, connected relationships help us say yes to opportunities, yes to embracing resources, yes to pursuing work that matters, yes to healthy people, yes to our talents, yes to serving mankind, yes to a beautiful family, yes to God, yes to everything that elevates meaningful living. They do this overtly and also simply with their sustained presence in our lives, because just being loved and knowing we belong is powerful fuel for a purposeful existence. When we have a crew, they have an unbelievable effect on our wholeness.

The second relates to adversity. Here, positive support not only buffers us from negative effects of stress but also helps us flourish because of or in spite of our circumstances. The difference between suffering alone or suffering while surrounded cannot be overstated. Those paths are so divergent, the experiences can't even be compared. Connectedness forges resiliency in our souls, and its accrued effect results in stronger, healthier, braver humans. We are all going to suffer, but togetherness is more powerful than pain.

In short, close relationships are *the key* to a meaningful life and the antidote to sorrow.

I am the collector of thousands of your stories. I couldn't begin to number how many women have shared pieces of their lives at conferences, across a book table, online, in the church lobby, over a meal, or on a plane. One common thread I hear over and over is this: *I want to be more connected and less lonely.* Of course this beats in so many of our hearts; it is literally our core need. I hear it from women who've moved and lost their squad, who've changed communities, who are trying to find their way into a group, a neighborhood, a church, a sisterhood. I hear it from women who've been burned and are scared to try again. From women whose marriages are the source of loneliness. From women who don't fit the norms that make it easier to connect in some places. From women who appear spit-shined on the outside but are actually deeply isolated. From women who didn't grow up in a healthy home life but want desperately to create one now.

This is a central need women tend to stay silent about. For some reason, loneliness breeds shame, and we are embarrassed to admit how hungry we are for connected relationships while blaming ourselves for the vacuum. Even though belonging is literally a primary need for every living human, we often feel alone in our loneliness and reluctant to make the necessary advances to change the story. These are the typical excuses that keep us in our silos:

Everyone already has a crew.
No one has time for me.
No one wants to make time for me.
I'm lonely because something is wrong with me.
I'm lonely because I'm not lovable.
Wanting connection is asking too much.
This is going to be too much work.
My bad history with relationships is insurmountable.
Women are mean.
Women are competitive.
I'm going to be disappointed.
I'm going to be disappointing.
I don't need close relationships.

Familiar? We talk ourselves out of vulnerability with excuses that, while sometimes true, are not always true and are not deal breakers. Some of them are outright lies. These are paltry reasons to remain lonely. Look at it this way: connected relationships *are* work, so make your peace with that. Yes, women can be mean and competitive, but you're telling me every woman in your zip code is a terror? Nope. And heads up: you *will* be disappointed at some point inside a meaningful relationship, and you absolutely *will* disappoint them. If bad experiences always indicate that your "picker is broken," like my friend Jamie says, then none of us would be connected at all because everyone has had a rotten relationship.

And listen, belonging is not asking too much, and you do need it.

Vibrant relationships are *essential* not just to your well-being but also your ability to cope, capacity for resiliency, pursuit of purpose, and likelihood of success. Guys, a study published in *Forbes* found overwhelming data that a lonely person is more likely to die early by around 30 percent, and when considering all the negative physiological effects, social isolation is a more significant health risk factor than smoking, obesity, exercise, and nutrition.[3]

The lonelier we are, the worse we are doing in every single facet.

The more connected we are, the better we are doing in every single facet.

So, yes, this matters. Yes, this is worth your time. Yes, this is worth the risk. Don't be your own jailer.

For a decade as a speaker, I traveled alone. I worked alone, I stayed in hotels alone, I ate alone, I carried the emotional and spiritual responsibility of the content alone, I managed new people and event staff alone, I taught alone. The weight was, in short, a crush. I distinctly remember looking at my calendar just before travel season and brimming with despair. All I could see was miles of empty pavement. In *Braving the Wilderness*, Brené Brown perfectly describes this as *the lonely feeling*:

> I can't tell you the number of times I've called Steve from the road and said, "I've got the lonely feeling." It's not unusual for Ellen or Charlie to say, "I don't like that restaurant. It gives me the lonely feeling," or, "Can my friend spend the night here? Her house gives me the lonely feeling." When the four of us tried to drill down on what "the lonely feeling" meant for our family, we all agreed that we get the lonely feeling in places that don't feel alive with connection.[4]

Brené's is a critical definition, because we can very much be surrounded by people and still feel lonely. This felt so familiar that, when I read it, I gasped. It's that weird internal empty feeling where everything feels wrong.

Likewise, being alone does not always equal loneliness. As a card-carrying introvert, alone time is my Promised Land. I will pay large amounts of American cash to be by myself, because I am awesome company and get to watch what I want and eat my own snacks and not ask myself a million questions. Yes and thank you. Being alone on my own terms is literally my favorite thing. Loneliness, on the other hand, typically happens when I am surrounded by people that aren't my people. They are nice people, good people, even dear people, but they aren't mine and I'm not theirs. They are connected to each other, but I am the "special guest" who still has to take a dozen cleansing breaths before walking into a room where I am warmly welcomed but, literally, unknown.

It is hard to describe the toll that decade of isolated travel took on me, on my family. That consistent loneliness put such strain on everything else. My resiliency, creativity, enthusiasm, clarity—it all took a hit. My stomach can feel it right now in memory. I would come home so depleted and desperate for connection, I would actually be a monster for two days. (Brandon and the kids would back this up, man.) The ferocious roar in my head would finally subside after a night or two at home, and I would land back in real life like someone who just emerged from a coma. I wasn't self-aware enough to suss out the source of the lonely feeling, so I mistakenly assumed it was the work itself and spent years trying to figure out how to do my job without traveling.

And then.

I traveled as part of a speaking team for the first time on the final season of the Women of Faith Tour, then experienced the group dynamic of the Belong Tour the following year, the Moxie

Matters Tour the next year and a half, the Tell Me More Tour with Kelly Corrigan, then the Hot Summer Nights (But Not That Hot) Tour with Heather Land. I was just one girl in a group of wild women, and we conquered every event together. Ladies and gentlemen, the Moxie crew traveled together on an actual tour bus and, one hysterical night after our event in Knoxville, ended up at a sketchy reggae spot called Bar Marley where we sang nineties karaoke until 2:30 a.m. as *the only eleven people in the room*. What in the world. I lay in my bus bunk that night and laughed for thirty minutes before I could fall asleep.

I cannot explain how much working with a team improved my mental health, evaporated my loneliness, and increased my joy. It felt like an honest-to-goodness miracle I never believed possible, so acute was my previous homesickness. Reader, please note that *I was doing the exact same work*. I didn't change *what* I was doing but *how* and *with whom*. Turns out, it wasn't the speaking bankrupting my reserves, nor was it my second-place scapegoat, travel itself, although both are taxing for sure. It was the loneliness.

This shift to teamwork changed my life. I come home full instead of empty, and I no longer need two days before I stop terrorizing my family. It is possible to be at home anywhere when you are alive with connection. This is real.

Straight up: we are better together. I don't believe any other theory. Whatever it is you do, pull some other folks into your work and see if it doesn't boost a dozen other levels on your flow chart. Collaborate, partner, share the microphone, invite contributors, support someone else's work, join forces, dream together, build something with colleagues, run your race with friends.

If you are feeling particularly lonely, perhaps in one specific area, I wonder if you might consider a way to invite more people into that thing: your work, your life, your community, your calling, your company, your parenting, your goals, your struggles, your faith, your favorite thing that should be so life-giving yet confusingly feels lonely. Good company might be the secret ingredient that makes the recipe finally work. It might not be the thing that's wrong; it might be the loneliness.

This requires you saying out loud what you are feeling on the inside, and that of course is vulnerable. Maria Popova wrote in *Figuring,* "Whatever we may mean by the word 'love,' we earn the right to use it only by doing the hard work of knowing and being known."[5] There is no other way, no shortcut. Intimacy requires vulnerability to manifest as anything beyond shallow connection. You have to show up like the real person you are. You have to say, "I want to be closer. I want to build connection. I will bring my whole self to the table." That is the only way the magic happens.

There is this lovely phrase in Scripture that says, "deep calls to deep," and this has been profoundly true for me. All people want connection, and we have some sort of radar for finding one another out in the wild. We feel promising chemistry. We notice those blowing past the chitchat and offering something genuine. We are drawn to others through shared experiences. Sometimes we just make an educated guess about a person. The deepest part of us that craves human contact calls out, and, lo and behold, someone usually answers. Loneliness sometimes suggests that we need an enormous, established community (and occasionally we find that), but don't underestimate the power of one or two deeply authentic relationships. That's really all it takes to transform isolation into joy.

Let it be said: sometimes building community doesn't work right away. You may false start a few times. Occasionally your educated guess about someone turns out to be wrong, and you have to press the eject button. It might also take longer than you want. When my daughter started her freshman year in college, she immediately joined a crew with a lot of razzle dazzle and began taking the city by storm. About five weeks in, she called and said, "Mom, I think I misread the room. I actually don't fit this group or this . . . pace. I am more Texan than I thought. I'm scared I missed the window to find my people." We talked about how to find her real squad, mainly where to look, key signals to watch for, red flags to pay attention to. It took her a semester and a half to find the fun, silly, slightly wholesome girls she didn't see in the first round. (Young mamas, "slightly wholesome" is the best-case scenario for your college kid, so be prepared to *lower the bar*.)

Two scenarios where loneliness seems to spike are: 1) in transition, and 2) in young motherhood, and sometimes these overlap. Transitions manifest in several ways. Sometimes it looks like life-stage shifts: from college to young adulthood, single to married, married to divorced, no kids to baby life, career world to stay-at-home world or vice versa, empty-nesterhood. These transitions cause our systems and rhythms to wobble, and the residual effects can alter not just our needs but our relationships. When the first woman in your circle has a baby, the equilibrium changes for everyone. When the SAHM goes back to school or work, the whole family fluctuates. When you send your last kid to college, you need new things from your community.

Worth noting is how these ancillary transitions usually take us by surprise. We fully understand that "going back to work" is going to change our schedule, but the relational shifts can be unexpected. When your stage in life changes in a fairly dramatic way, it deeply affects the relationships forged in the previous stage, even dear ones. You need new support, new understanding, new shared experiences, new counsel. This doesn't necessarily mean you create a whole different crew, but you might need to add some folks into rotation who understand the challenges or additions or subtractions this fresh season brings. (I have a home squad that could care less about my public life and a career squad that understands every weird thing about it.) All of this is normal, so don't feel like you are failing your OG group or they are failing you. Some friends are lifers, some are seasonal, and a precious few are both.

Other transitions are geographical. I've learned a lot from the military members and wives in my reader community. With such frequent relocations and deployments, they literally have to build their own troop. These girls have it down. What I notice is how they ignore all the excuses I listed earlier. They waste zero seconds worrying if someone is going to reciprocate their invitation or make room for them or be a good fit. They don't have time for that. They are nowhere near their own parents or siblings, they are in states they didn't grow up in, they or their spouses may not be in the country, and they have a whole life to manage. Military women show up to new stations like, "WHERE MY PEOPLE AT?" Consequently, they have some of the most connected, inter-dependent, loyal communities I've ever seen.

Besides transition, it should be said that motherhood, particularly with littles, is where my community often feels isolated. "The injustice is this," wrote Beth Berry,

> It takes a village, but there are no villages. By village I don't simply mean "a group of houses and associated buildings, larger than a hamlet and smaller than a town, situated in a rural area." I'm referring to the way of life inherent to relatively small, relatively contained multigenerational communities. Communities within which individuals know one another well, share the joys, burdens, and sorrows of everyday life, nurture one another in times of need, mind the well-being of each other's ever-roaming children and increasingly dependent elderly, and feel fed by their *clearly* essential contribution to the group that securely holds them. I'm talking about the most natural environment

for children to grow up in. I'm talking about a way of life we are biologically wired for, but that is nearly impossible to find in developed nations. I'm talking about the primary unmet need driving the frustration that most every village-less mother is feeling.[6]

Individual parents are expected to make up for what entire communities used to provide. We have to create our own crew when we have the least time, energy, and bandwidth to do it. We try to fill in the gaps with social media, but that leaves us strangely even less connected. Plus, we feel the pressure to provide over-the-top, stimulating childhoods by spending money we don't have on activities our kids don't need, because the wild, rich, village-based childhood of yesteryear is over. Kids once roamed from house to house, building and inventing and creating and gallivanting. Then whatever mom or aunt was around at mealtime would feed them and send them back out, and they'd come home from their adventures with tales and scratches. Parents were connected, relatives were typically close by, and the village raised the children. This is how a great deal of the world still operates.

There are gorgeous current examples of village life at its finest, outposts of hope in a disconnected culture. In Newton, Massachusetts, journalist Thomas Farragher wrote,

Something small and profound is happening here along the banks of the Charles River. It's a love story. It's a story of a little girl who's deaf. It's a story of neighbors who've raised their own children and are now embracing a beautiful two-year-old named Samantha. It's a story of twenty neighbors who sit in silence to learn a new language so their littlest neighbor will know what their kids have always known: Community. Friendship. Inclusion.

And of Samantha's parents:

Their first hint of what would come next from their neighbors was in the way they were welcomed when they first moved to the neighborhood. There were plates of cookies. There were greetings from neighbors in kayaks, bearing the promises of friendship. This is a place where elderly neighbors' driveways are shoveled without prompting. If you're sick, expect a casserole. And now this: The new baby on the street was deaf. . . . These neighbors didn't ask Sam's parents' permission. They hired an instructor. And got started. As winter's grip tightened around New England the other night, Rhys McGovern, a hard-of-hearing speech language pathologist, went to work before a class of eighteen in Lucia Marshall's living room.[7]

Unthinkably beautiful.

So if you are parenting and feel impossibly lonely, exhausted, guilty, and anxious, know that you are being asked to accomplish a monumental task that has been a group project in every generation until now. You are doing a wonderful job. Seriously. And you are doing enough. Our cultural narrative is lying to you. You just need to find your village.

In order to begin re-villaging our communities, Berry suggested:

GET REALLY CLEAR ON ONE THING. The fact that you're struggling is not a reflection of your inadequacies but the unnatural cultural circumstances you're living within.

OWN + HONOR YOUR NEEDS. Most mothers are walking around with several deeply unmet needs of their own while focusing almost exclusively on the needs of others. This is precisely the thing that keeps us from gaining traction and improving our circumstances.

PRACTICE VULNERABILITY. Rich, safe, authentic connection is essential for thriving. Cultivating this quality of connection takes courage and a willingness to step outside your comfort zone. What you want most exists on the other side of that initial awkward conversation or embarrassing introduction. JUST DO IT.

OWN YOUR STRENGTHS. What makes you feel strong and fully alive? What lights you up and gives you energy just thinking about it? Who would you be to your village if you had one?

BECOME AN INTEGRAL PART OF SOMETHING. Whether it's a knitting group, dance troupe, church, kayaking club, or homeschool collective, commit to growing community around one area of your life that enlivens you or fills a need.

SPEAK YOUR TRUTH. Even when you're terrified. Even if it makes you the bravest one in the room.[8]

In my experience, motherhood became less lonely as the kids got older. When the physical crush of parenting littles receded, I found the challenges of middle kids and older kids more manageable. Of course, by that time I was a happy member of a tight community, and we rolled forward together through every new stage, so I'm not sure where to place the credit. But I will just say that sleeping through the night and not potty training is *helpful*. Easier days are ahead, young dears. Hang on to your squad; you guys will make it together.

It is good and important work to live a connected life. If this is the area where you concentrate your energy, it is time well spent. Without even direct correlations, a sense of real community will improve your mental health, resiliency, and productivity, like when you cut out dairy to alleviate stomach aches and discover your skin clears up too. Connectedness is powerful fuel for a creative, courageous life. It sets a beautiful example for our children, because we surely don't want to pass on the suggestion that they won't need anyone else to flourish.

And if you are hung up on fear—*this didn't work before, I don't want to be rejected, I don't know how to be in a healthy community, I don't like to be vulnerable*—I'll ask you this gently: How is your current life working for you? Is your loneliness better than taking a risk? Is your isolation the story you still want to be telling five years from now? Ten years from now? Is it possible that as a member of humanity literally built to crave relationships, you might not even have to look that hard? Would you consider that even making one genuine connection could radically improve your life?

Where can you start looking for connection? Here are some potential pools: your neighborhood, your kids' school, your workplace, church, the gym, book clubs, meet-up groups in your city (this is a real thing), activist groups, running clubs (omg, the only reason I know this is my friend Trina), support groups, any special-interest space (knitting, writing groups, cooking clubs, dog lovers), Bible study, playgroups, Bunco, professional networks, volunteer orgs. Guys, Brandon and I have a whole community built out of his biker gang. Okay, fine, it is a "motorcycle club," but my point is that we take weekend trips together and have Family Nights and community service projects and now have friends all over Texas who are bouncers, club owners, rogue accountants, and, in one case, a famous pottery artist. YOU NEVER KNOW.

One last word: to those of you in lucky possession of rich relationships *and* to those in dire need of them, please, I beg you, look around. People are so lonely, and they are everywhere. We have great power over the disconnection that plagues our culture. Our cities are full of new moms, just-moved-here folks, immigrants, new neighbors, people peeking their heads into church, relocated young adults apart from their families, refugees, college kids, new hires. They are also full of people who've lived there for a decade and still crave more connection. Throw open your home. Invite a new friend to coffee, to playgroup, to book club, to dinner. Plan a neighborhood block party. Reach out to the immigrant and refugee community in your city (these mamas are so lonely and starving for friends). Widen your circle. Ask someone to Bible study. Organize a Girls' Night Out. Send a quick text.

Like I wrote in *For the Love* on the prison of loneliness:

> We have the keys, you guys! They look like tables and couches, beef stew and crusty French bread. They include patio chairs and music, football on the TV and cold beer. They involve a simple email invite for Friday night and burgers on the grill. They say, bring your kids and we'll lock them all in the back-yard with popsicles. The keys include good questions and good listening around a fire pit; they certainly contain stories and laughter. They don't require fussing or fluffing much, so don't let those stop you, because a messy kitchen only tells me someone cares enough to feed me, which is a good key. Instead of waiting for community, provide it, and you'll end up with it anyway.[9]

We are the antidote to so much isolation. Developing eyes to see loneliness and hands to reach out is one of our greatest gifts to the world. I believe God uses us to meet the most common, primal need shared in every community on earth: belonging. It is more powerful than ten thousand other best practices. Creating safe spaces for others to be seen and loved and known and celebrated is the height of goodness and the solution to so much sadness.

Don't cover up your loneliness with busyness or success or feigned indifference. Don't keep this need buried. Pull this one straight into the light, take a deep breath, and suggest to two or three friends that you buy matching obnoxious sweatshirts. If they bite, those weirdos are yours.

WHAT I WANT

7

I WANT THIS DREAM

I worked methodically, even maniacally, for a few years to engineer a complete relocation of my entire family to Austin where we alone lived. Our people were in Kansas and Oklahoma and Colorado, and we were the sole defectors to Texas way back in 1998. I had a bunch of babies growing up without grandparents and aunts and uncles and I missed my crew—and also Austin is the actual best—so Brandon and I started a campaign. It involved propaganda, very slight manipulation, and a healthy dose of applied FOMO (Fear Of Missing Out) when useful.

Short story: our entire family moved to Austin. Both sets of our parents and all our sibs and their families.

We did it! Respect our prowess!

The commune was complete and making all my dreams come true: family barbecues, Sunday dinners, football watch parties, casual sleepovers. Having raised my littles alone for years, it was everything I ever wanted. Then came a day in 2010 when my sister

Lindsay, the very first migrant to Austin, told the rest of us she was leaving her steady office career and moving to New York City, New York, America, to attend culinary school (wth) and start a new kind of life. We were crushed.

It is horrifying to remember the pressure we put on her to reconsider a happy life in the one we liked her in ("Think of the family!"). We activated a tsunami of despair, disapproval, discouragement, and displeasure. *Stay here!* we cried. *We need you and want you here!* Thank goodness she had the fortitude to ignore our family peer pressure and move to the Big City. She went to school and started a whole new career as a chef, leaving corporate America for the heat and hiss of the kitchen. Spoiler alert: she moved back to Austin nine years later and is cheffing in the ATX because God is real.

That I, a bona fide Dream Believer™, would discourage *my own sister's goals* tells me that we are in for a real fight here. This is one of those conversations sometimes easier to imagine in someone else's life. *Your* goals and dreams? Outstanding! Go for it! Chase it down! You are a champion! Now, someone very close to me? Hmmm. How will this affect me? Will this cost me something? What if they fail? These stakes feel higher. My *own* dream? How dare I. Impossible. Terrifying. Selfish. No.

And yet. Women are absolutely seeded with bright ideas, audacious goals, creative gifts begging to be brought forth. We have big thoughts. We see paths we are positively made to walk on. We want something big or beautiful or new or exciting. Pretending we don't care or squashing our own instincts toward a dream doesn't mean it isn't still humming under the surface, jumping up and down to be noticed and named, begging for permission to materialize in our lives.

Can we discuss the word *want* briefly? Women have been discouraged from hunger in general. Having a big, healthy appetite for something doesn't easily line up with our historical role inside the patriarchy. We are not supposed to want like this. Approved wants: whatever your husband wants, the desires of your children, whatever the community needs, the sanctioned wants of your specific subculture. Our wants have a complicated system of checks and balances: Does this seem too greedy? Will this cost the people around me something? Is this selfish? Is this too ambitious? How long can I chase this before I have to revert?

I am never entirely sure how unique the Christian community is inside the greater community of women, but it feels like Women Who Want endure outsized critique under the steeples. Our lady roles are more heavily cemented inside the "God sanctioned" patriarchy, so our wants are limited by bad theology, gender complementarianism, and communal disapproval. In many cases, women are literally not allowed to preach or lead the church at large, so if their want is attached to spiritual authority, they are plumb out of luck. But even south of pulpit dreams, women are expected to supply the grease for the engine, not the fuel. We are meant to serve and submit, defer and support. Ambition is suspect—a sure sign of a prideful heart not rendered to the Lord. "She is of the world," the weird Christian rhetoric often concludes.

I present as evidence that prick of fear or judgment poking its head out of your worldview as we speak, Christian reader. That one that might be saying, "I mean, have some dreams, sure, but . . ." or "Yes, but we really *are* called to . . ." May I submit that having your own dream does not for one millisecond cancel out service to our families, great love for our neighbors, concern for the poor, or a heart for the world. It does not require practices in opposition to your faith. Ambition does not mean you are now the sole recipient of your life's energy. It doesn't ask you to abandon your core personality for a caricature of a Boss Babe. God would not craft our minds and hands to make beautiful things, then shame us for wanting to. You will never convince me that passion is anything short of godly. Never.

Listen, you have the right to dream a dream.

I cannot imagine a brighter world than one in which every human is alive with energy, released into his or her greatest dreams, contributing, creating, inventing, thriving. I suspect any problem yet unsolved on earth is only because so many of its glorious humans are silenced by gender limitations, poverty, oppression, and white supremacy. Were every mind unleashed without obstruction, can you imagine how the world would be flourishing? How many solutions, innovations, and developments would exist? We are operating at half-capacity at best. By elevating a few at the expense of the rest, humanity is its own worst enemy, shooting itself in the foot.

This brings me to you. If you have a secret dream, a private desire, and you are refusing to bring it into the light of day, we actually need you. Have you considered that? Have you thought about what wonderfulness you are meant to bring to bear on this earth? There is an empty void right where your talent belongs. Literally nobody else can do what you do in the way you do it. What? Someone already wrote your book? Opened your business? Started your ministry? Created your art? Horsecrap. No one has done your work already, because they couldn't possibly. If you are waiting to find the first dream never before attempted, built, or created, I'd like to introduce you to a little thing called The World Is Big and Stuff Has Been Done Already But There Is Still Room for You Because the World Is Big As I Mentioned.

Call from child at a sleepover:

Child: Mom, I know YOU don't like them, but we want to watch a scary movie. Can I? I am not scared.

Me: Oh, you aren't? You know in advance you won't be scared? What movie?

Child: *The Conjuring.* Everyone here has already seen it
and they all agree that it should be PG-13, but for
some reason it is rated R.

Me: Wow. Those movie executives really biffed on
this one. How dare they mislabel a movie so
middle school kids can't watch it. I wonder how
they got this so wrong. Maybe y'all can write
them your thoughts on the PG-13 scam.

Child: Mom, you don't sound very positive.

Me: Well, I'm just upset at this industry that can't
properly label a scary movie about devils. I guess
you better find another movie to watch.

Child: (earnestly) *Mom, I only have one life to live.*
You don't know how long I have. What if I die
tomorrow, Mom, and I never saw this movie?
What if this is my last day?

Me: Well, that would be real, real sad. I guess you'd
go to heaven without seeing it. Maybe there is
Netflix up there.

(Jesus, receive the middle schoolers in your arms. They are
under severe persecution down here. Everyone is against them: the
Hollywood movie raters, the parents, time itself. They all may be
gone from this earth tomorrow having not experienced life to the
fullest, and they need your presence, God. Comfort them in their
distress.)

Dear reader, YOU ONLY HAVE ONE LIFE TO LIVE. What
if you die tomorrow having never given your dream a shot? What
if you let fear or disapproval keep you sidelined without leaving it all on the table? Think of the goodness you are sitting on.
Whatever your dream, it is worth your participation. Just scanning
my office, the books on my shelves, the art on my walls, the music

on my speaker, the furniture built by hand, the aesthetic inspired by gifted designers, I am utterly grateful these people said yes to their dreams; my life is so much richer, wiser, more beautiful, more delightful for their immense gifts. Thank you, Yes People! I am the lucky recipient of your talents. Thank you for *wanting*.

Dreams are obviously not limited. They don't only count if they are audacious, and they're not unreachable if they are. Surveying my little world, my in-real-life people said yes or are in the process of saying yes to the following dreams: starting a daily Facebook live, becoming foster parents, getting yoga certified at forty-five, starting a retirement-planning firm (staff: two, married, *be near, Jesus*), taking Spanish classes at fifty-one, opening a food pantry, scaling a midwifery practice, running a half marathon, opening an Etsy shop, reforming the foster system nationwide, downsizing to tiny home living, becoming an online stylist, trying stand-up comedy. Dreams come in every shape and size. They are creative, cerebral, corporate; physical, mental, spiritual; from scratch, in flux, plug and play; require education, practice, mentoring; and could be a side hustle, part-time, or a full-time leap.

They can look any which way, but you are in charge of bringing yours forth. Why are we so weird about this sometimes? This aw-shucks-how-dare-I thing is debilitating. If you don't even believe in your own capacity, your own right to imagine, how will anyone else? You will likely need to call on your people as you start the engine, so at least give them the confidence that you are all in. Other folks can rarely *believe you* across the finish line; that is your work. Don't give away your power by requiring the community to do your heavy lifting. They won't care as much, want it as badly, envision it correctly, stick with it long enough. Why should they? I mean this gently, but other people don't have time to make your aspirations come to life.

Now, might they encourage you? Make a good connection for

you? Support you? Believe in you? Oh, my stars, absolutely. I would be light years behind without my squad. There is no way to explain how crucial their support roles have been. Everything I've put my hand to has a dozen other fingerprints on it. Some of my people are full-time teammates, some collaborators, some advisors, and some just cheerleaders. Their contributions range from signed-in-blood partnerships to seasonal, short-term investors. I've been handed a single sentence that changed my trajectory (Thank you, kind stranger!) and also had people remain on my ship even when it sunk for a minute, those loyal dreamboats. I am not a self-made woman, which, as I mentioned earlier, is not a thing.

But the fire in the belly, the late nights, the zero paychecks, the commitment, the thousands of hours logged in obscurity—those were mine. I clung to a vision for my life well past its due date. When I should've hung it up and gotten a real job (a "real job" being one that paid money), I stayed the course. I put my head down and worked so hard for so many years while also working hard on everything else. When early results could be interpreted no other way than "failure," I refused to take no for an answer. Why?

I just knew this *want* of mine was going somewhere.

I had already said yes—to Jesus, to myself, to the women I served—and I refused to grab the low-hanging fruit of overnight success stories, easy eject buttons, or career-ending discouragement ("career" here being a very loose term). I have always found work very noble, and I considered it an honor to show up for my own life in a way I would be proud of later. I never wanted to look back and admit I'd gone half-assed into my calling, giving up at the first rejection, the early wobbles. If none of it ever took flight, it wouldn't be because I didn't commit and persist. I was going big and not going home.

Got a dream? Show up for it.

Assemble your squad, and then hit step one: say it out loud.

It's powerful, this vulnerable move. Now it's real. You've put some language around it, pulled it into the light. That inside dream just got born on the outside where people can see it. You've given it the respect it deserves by naming it, assigning it some heft, breathing life into its lungs. This is not a small step.

I remember explicitly the day back in 2004 I told Brandon I wanted to write a book. It was March, and according to my Spawning Cycle, it was my summer to have another baby after popping them out in April 1998, May 2000, and June 2002. Reader, we were drowning in toddlers and preschoolers, and I was watching other people's kids part-time to the tune of around $150 a week. Brandon was working eleven million hours while storing the notion that I was *surely* about to return to the classroom. He'd walk in the door every day and find his formerly lovely, kempt, stable wife sporting the same sloppy clothes I woke up in, bedraggled hair, children hanging off all my parts, and a wild, desperate look on my face I now recognize with perfect clarity on moms shopping with their littles at Target. I actually can't believe he ever drove home after work. Our life was a literal shit show.

So, to this mix of early childhood, financial instability, and zero margin, I whispered, "Instead of having another baby this summer, I think I'll . . . write a book."

Dear ones, at this juncture, let's talk about possible reactions to your announcement. Sometimes your thing will make neither hide nor hair of sense. It will sound absurd. (For example, you may want to write a book and not even have a computer. Also, no one is asking you to write a book, so there is that.) Or maybe it's just that so many people live in your home, adding a new thing feels somewhere between hilarious and psychotic. Perhaps someone expected you to take a different path, or rejoin a former one, or make a choice with a more guaranteed outcome. Those who love us aren't keen on our failure or rejection, and their fear for us sometimes shows up as discouragement. It could be that your idea is going to cost not just you but your people something (right on both counts), and they will feel anxious about this development. Let it be said that folks probably prefer you to keep doing exactly what you are doing so as not to interrupt their lives, and it is not because your people are monsters; they are just monster-adjacent, as we all are.

Another potential pool of reactions involves old-fashioned jealousy, or its cousin, self-loathing. The thing is, we all have dreams, everyone has a gift, human beings are literally wired for lives of meaning, so occasionally your ambition will rub up against someone else's dormant desire and that feels bad to them. Your forward movement reminds them of their own stagnation, so an easy shot is to say you are a big dummy, a try-hard, conceited, doomed to fail. Notice you won't typically receive that response from people neck deep in their own awesome stuff; those guys will be pumped for you. When folks are running their own race, they are thrilled to see other runners lace up their shoes. It's the ones in the camp chairs on the sidelines with a Natty Light booing the new runners and hoping you'll get disqualified. How much power do you want to hand over to *those* guys?

While it is good to be prepared for any number of reactions, decide in advance that you are not asking for permission. You may appropriately be open to feedback but not dismissal. This is a huge part of becoming an integrated woman. You have agency over your own life, and it is not up for grabs. Obviously, be willing to receive good counsel or strategic advice or useful suggestions as to your path forward, but that does not include handing your dream over for rejection. It isn't theirs to reject. It belongs to you, and you are its mother and father, its doting aunt and closest sister, its body-guard and lead blocker. Protect it in its undeveloped infant stage; who else will?

When I said my thing out loud—we're going to give Brandon loads of credit, folks—there was some ... big gulping, some ... loud nose breathing, some ... blank staring. Because let's call a spade a spade: this was the most outrageous thing I could have announced in the Year of Our Lord 2004. I might as well have said I was entering a female body-building contest for all the sense "writing a book" made. But he went out and bought a used laptop, plugged it into our dial-up internet, and helped rearrange our schedule so I could write a few hours a week without the spawn asking for fish sticks. By November, I had ten offers for that little book.

Back to you. You've said the thing out loud. People loved it or fainted. They joined your hype squad or caused you to drink a little. It took some maneuvering or fell right into place. Either way, time to put your money where your mouth went. In the rarest of cases, stepping into your new dream will cause very little turbulence. Occasionally, it just replaces something that already held open the time slot or the energy required. You get to do a swap-a-doodle and plug right in.

But typically this is the moment you realize, "Oh. I've done a thing here." You'll have to put some gas in the tank. These early steps may include but are not limited to: research, exposure, brave requests, strategic emails, new classes, workshops, purchasing materials, up-front financial investments, joining professional groups, calendar reorganizing, jettisoning some prior commitments, observation trips, a million YouTube tutorials, market research, skill development, important conversations, information compilation. I believe another term for all this is "hard work."

I want to build a tiny home and move my family off the grid.

I want to open a flower shop with nothing but tulips.

I want to go back to college to learn robotics.

I want to be a painter like Jack in *Titanic*.

I want to live in London for a year.

I want to build a mobile dog-grooming van.

I want to be a songwriter for Kelly Clarkson.

I want to turn my garage into a neighborhood library.

I want to run for office.

I want to learn guitar and start a garage band of moms.

I want to build an org against human trafficking.

I want to retire five years early.

I want to RV across America for a year.

I want to teach English in Japan.

I love your dreams! I love your wild, amazing ideas. I love how you are wired and the stuff that fires your engine. I love how your eyes light up and you start talking too fast. But guess what? You gotta work for this. Everything you want is on the other side of hard. Shonda Rhimes put it like this: "I understand a dream job is not about dreaming—it's all job, all work, all reality, all blood, all sweat, no tears."[1] Well, *maybe a few tears, Shonda,* but all that work isn't just a means to the end; it is a precious asset in and of itself. Those hours, all the conversations, the learning, the setbacks, the stuff before results—this builds something strong in you you'll need for the long haul. You find out what you're made of when no one is watching, much less applauding.

I won't belabor the point I've already made, but I became an overnight success in just under a decade. I regret nothing. Those years taught me how to write and gave me time to find my voice. They showed me how to receive one-half of one golf clap for my work. I learned to take criticism and editorial direction without breaking out my voodoo dolls. Those years gave me the runway to examine my own worldview, my real theology. I would like to thank Baby Jesus in the Manger that none of y'all read my early work. Purge the shelves of that drivel, Messiah! I was but a wee babe! I got to laser focus on the craft of writing, because I didn't have to give any energy to things like "selling any books" or "managing success" or "crushing social media." There was no Facebook or Twitter or Instagram when I started! We published books the old-fashioned way: by activating our mind power to control book buyers. It didn't work. Thank you for attending my Ted Talk.

Do not disparage the clunky beginnings. Treat your early steps as seriously as if the whole world was watching, a crucial part of the process to be proud of later. Remember why you care, why you want this, because discouragement lurks abundantly here. Even your early adopters can flounder if it takes longer than expected or goes sideways for a while. Failure will be there to potentially derail your dream—that is, only if you think failure can't be your best teacher, which it can and it is. You might look at someone a few miles ahead of you in a similar lane and decide you are too far behind. Or you might see someone who started after you bypass you, and despair and jealousy seeps in. This is a pile of garbage. Don't fall for it. There is enough, enough, enough. There is enough business for all, creativity for all, big ideas for all, innovation for all. No one is stealing from anybody. Just put your head down and do your work.

For some, this is a total reboot. You are an accountant who wants to open a panini shop. You have never lived anywhere but Missouri and want to buy a little cottage on the coast of Oregon. You want to try a half-marathon but haven't run since seventh grade P.E. You are neck deep in mothering but want to develop a mentoring program for high school girls from scratch. You want to speak French, but your only experience is eating croissants. Some dreams will clear the deck and escort you straight to the drawing board.

This gets me excited for you. Time to learn! Learning is underrated. We are surrounded by success stories and finished products.

It seems like everyone is already at the party. But the humble process of starting at the very beginning of a skill, a space, a craft, an industry—this is the stuff that wakes your mind up and makes you feel alive. My girlfriend Jenny literally googled, "Is 51 too old to learn a language? Can my brain still do it?" GOOGLE SAID IT COULD. So she downloaded an entire Spanish course and is working her way through the lessons. As of this writing, she is utterly terrible because she is from country-fried chicken Alabama (all she does is repeatedly ask us our names and where we are from in Español), but you know what? She laced up her shoes, she took the first few steps, she is running the race. *Muy bien!*

One of my favorite shows is *Chef's Table* on Netflix. Each episode has the same story arc. You can almost set a clock to it. Fifteen minutes of backstory, five minutes on what attracted the chef to cooking, ten minutes of Hard Knocks™, then inspiration plus talent followed by success plus accolades. But regardless of their cuisine or location, no matter how natural their ability or refined their palate, whether they were a recipient of some luck or investors or rich family members, *all* of them have to know how to bone a chicken, fillet a fish, make a roux, strain a stock. They started at culinary school, not at *Chef's Table*. Their hands and arms are a map of scars, evidence of the work, the cost, the irreplaceable edge from paying their dues.

If you are staring down a dream that requires fresh, brand-new knowledge you are not yet in possession of, take heart. The very best among us had to learn too. Google says you can do this! You can learn anything. The only question is, do you really want to? This is that inside you/outside you integrated work. If you sincerely want something in your heart, feed it well and let it grow, sister. So much potential exists.

Dr. Carol Dweck explained the difference between feeling stuck and believing in possibility using the terms *fixed mindset* and *growth mindset*. In her book, *Mindset: The New Psychology for Success*, she wrote: "For twenty years, my research has shown that the view you adopt for yourself profoundly affects the way you lead your life." Sara Robinson wrote, "When we believe that the qualities we have cannot be changed, that they are set in stone, we have a fixed mindset. With this mindset, we are likely to believe that change is impossible and we are stuck with what we are "given."[2]

In other words, a fixed mindset means we believe our core personality, character, talent, abilities, and intelligence are locked. We are either smart or dumb. We are either gifted at something or we aren't. The world is made up of some talented people whom the rest admire from the sidelines. Here is a great clue while self-evaluating: Dweck found people with a fixed mindset feel the need to prove themselves over and over and evaluate themselves in an all-or-nothing way: "Will I succeed or fail? Will I look clever or stupid? Will I be accepted or rejected?"[3] It is a feast-or-famine, one hundred-or-zero, win-or-lose game, which isn't even how life works. There are a thousand gradations between all and none, and if we only expect "all" straight out of the gate, we will miss the spectacular forward process of "some." Just keep going.

The contrast to the fixed mindset is the growth mindset, which acknowledges that we start with a set of qualities, but they can be cultivated with effort and grow through application and experience. This doesn't mean we can all be geniuses or Olympians, but it does acknowledge potential. People with a growth mindset approach a situation understanding that, even if they falter at the start, they can improve. In short, everything about a person is malleable. So, there are no smart or dumb people—only those who decided to learn the ropes. There are not capable or incompetent people— only hard-working ones. You aren't doomed to the sidelines merely observing the game; you could join if you are willing to put in the effort. Just about anyone can learn to dance, garden, cook, write, paint, build, rewire a lamp, practice law, pick up German, speak publicly, start a nonprofit, make jewelry, exercise, create spreadsheets, podcast, teach the Bible, be a stylist, mix cocktails, fix an engine, tile a bathroom.[4]

Remember what we learned in the last chapter about human flourishing? The three pillars of emotional health via the Self-Determination Theory (SDT):

Autonomy (being in control of your own life)
Competence (being capable to succeed and thrive)
Relatedness (being in close personal relationships)

Although positive relatedness to some degree meets all three needs, do you see how important agency and competence matter to your life? Here is the bottom line: whatever your dream, you are capable and worthy of it. Whether it involves pulling a smaller lever in the larger scheme of your life or engineering a whole new mechanism, you can do it.

One, you literally *can* do it; you already have permission as a member of the human race. You don't have to ask for it. You can want what you want and go after it full throttle. It is so exciting, this thing you want. Thank goodness you care about it.

And two, you can *do* it. You are able. You can learn. You can practice. You can develop. You can figure it out. You can work hard. You can overcome the obvious challenges. You can pull this thing off if you stay the course. You have the chops.

Do it for your kids, who are watching. Do it for your community and colleagues and neighbors. Do it for Jesus, if he indeed compels you. Do it for your family. Do it for the people your work will serve, encourage, inspire, include. Do it for a culture that is disintegrated right now and needs some good news. Dreams realized are such a joy to the world. Do it for the justice, beauty, truth, or freedom on the other side. And finally, do it for yourself, you wonderful, deserving, magnificent person. What a gift you are.

8

I WANT TO CHOOSE MY YESES

We have five kids, because no one told us not to do that. I had three the way you have them, like out of your body, then we adopted our youngest two from Ethiopia when they were eight and five. There are a million of them, and they are always talking, and everyone has Large Feelings, and sometimes it feels like *Lord of the Flies* up in here. Big families know you spend the majority of your energy just getting people fed, shuttled, moderately showered, and kept out of jail. When I see a small family sitting in a restaurant eating quietly, it literally confuses my brain: *What is happening? I don't understand. Why aren't they talking over each other? Why is no one arguing? I demand answers.*

In our quagmire of drama, one-on-one time with each kid is hard to come by. So when our oldest was approaching thirteen, Brandon and I created a family tradition: every freshly minted thirteen-year-old gets a surprise trip with one parent. They don't know when or where. We pulled one out of bed at 4:30 a.m. for a flight to New York City. We showed up to middle school with packed bags for another. We told one he was going to soccer practice and drove him straight to the airport, Colorado bound. They are on pins and needles for two weeks leading up to their birthdays, wild with anticipation.

We tuck letters from all the important people in their lives into our bags. Their aunts and grandmas, pastors and teachers, uncles and grandpas, bonus parents and coaches. Over the course of each trip, we hand over the letters one at a time, spreading out the love and mentorship. As someone who once threw all her children's dirty clothes in the backyard like a crazed nutter, this is one of my few shining moments.

Out of the gate, Brandon and I decided these adventures were "Yes Trips." Yes to the side of fries with your pasta, yes to dinner at 10:30 p.m., yes to Gavin hiking up a steep waterfall Mom would say no to, yes to swimming at midnight, yes to two desserts, yes to three hours at H&M in Times Square with Sydney (fix it, Jesus), yes to room service, yes to crazy pictures, yes to Ben playing chess in Bryant Park with strangers, yes to carriage rides, yes to outrageous silliness, yes to Remy getting her eyebrows waxed at Saks Fifth Avenue, yes to Coke for breakfast, yes to it all. There is a time for restraint and normal rules, and the Yes Trips are not it. They are permissive and extravagant in a very thirteen-year-old way, and they compose some of my kids' greatest childhood memories.

This when-to-say-yes-and-when-to-say-no thing is no joke with real consequences. Adult life is chock-full of these choices. It is a war between a myriad of shoulds, shouldn'ts, won'ts, don't want tos, wish I coulds, I guess I wills, and do I have tos. The average woman is presented with one thousand choices for every one hundred slots. Waiting in the wings to accompany each reluctant yes or apologetic no is resentment, exhaustion, unproductiveness, and guilt. As with everything else we've discussed, there is a real cost to ceding ownership here. Making reluctant choices that don't reflect our actual desires is a major breach; we have to work hard on integration here. We must steer our own ship or risk capsizing under too many waves or becoming lost at sea.

Let's talk about yeses first. Yeses are fun, or at least they certainly can be. Who doesn't want to make room for a few metaphorical Yes Trips in her life? When chosen carefully, a well-placed *yes* can be the best decision of your life. The right yeses can completely, utterly, fantastically change your trajectory. Google's executive chairman said it best during his commencement address at the University of California at Berkeley:

> Find a way to say yes to things. Say yes to invitations to a new country. Say yes to meeting new friends. Say yes to learning a new language, picking up a new sport. Yes is how you get your first job, and your next job. Yes is how you find your spouse, and even your kids. Even if it's a bit edgy, a bit out of your comfort zone, saying yes means you will do something new, meet someone new and make a difference in your life, and likely in others' lives as well.... Yes is a tiny word that can do big things.

Power of Positivity.com further encouraged:

> Say it often. Saying yes requires work, commitment and accountability, and sometimes that scares people away, especially if they feel unprepared or unmotivated. But here's the reality: a yes will always give you more than a no. A no is guaranteed failure. Nothing is ever stagnant, so a no is usually backward progress. Sure, there is no risk in a no, but there's no fun in it either. Saying yes can be very fun. In the fun is where you find success.[1]

I like this. Some of my greatest memories and successes have been just on the other side of a yes. Admittedly, some of us are simply wired for enthusiasm. Enneagram Sevens, for example, were put on this earth to experience BIG YES LIVES. I parent a Seven, and she once told me: "Mom, do you know what my greatest fear is? That, despite all my dreams, I will end up working in a cubicle. I can't even watch office shows, Mom. They make me feel dark inside." Well, God bless America. Some of us will find yeses easier than others (but will likely struggle with the nos, which we'll get to).

For the rest of us, sometimes we start with our desired endgame, then back up and determine the yeses that will get us there. What do you want? Where do you want to go? What simple yeses will move you toward your goal? I find these incremental steps challenging, because I am a Big Idea type. Me to my team: *Let's start a killer book club! I want to do a live podcast tour! Let's build a network! I have ideas for a subscription box!* I have natural vision for finished products, but every one of them requires a hundred appropriate yeses to get there. These steps are far less sexy than the grand release, the big finale, but without them, the Big Idea is only an unrealized concept I was excited about once. A million people get stuck here, because the necessary yeses feel too hard or too slow or too unlikely. Imagine your yeses as dominoes; just tip that first one. Maybe it is simply a conversation, an introduction, a meeting, a download. It is your first yes, not your only. That first yes is a biggie.

We typically feel stuck, locked into our previous yeses or those that are immutable, but the truth is, most of our tasks have a degree of flex. They do. Let's not bog down in a straw man argument here ("Well, who is going to do my laundry? I can't choose not to *parent*, Jen Hatmaker."). Can we discuss our choices in a reasonable way, agreeing that parts of our lives are obviously immovable, if only for this season? I'm not suggesting you outsource motherhood or give up adulting like a normal person. Clearly, portions of every adult life include boring, mundane tasks that have to get done. We also have to pay our bills; we don't get to Marie Kondo our entire lives. Doing taxes will never spark joy, yet here they are every March, screwing up our mojo. Parts of life require yeses, because we are not billionaire moguls who get to self-select only our favorite enterprises.

Having said that, other parts are more fluid. They are not absolute. They can be shifted or eliminated or created from scratch. Often the notion that something is rigid indicates a lack of imagination. It may also be a defense mechanism to the suspected reactions of others. When a new yes is guaranteed to draw a critique from those your shifting trajectory will affect, a natural response is to declare the whole operation dead in the water so you don't have to manage their criticism.

But look closer. Other people's frustration won't kill you. Their opinions can't take you out. You can indeed choose a new yes, or a continued yes. You can keep at the thing you love, even if it isn't producing results yet. You can say yes to what you want to say yes to. Is it giving you life? Is it making your brain sizzle in a good way? Is it stretching your creativity? Is it filling your tank? Is it serving the people you want to serve? Is it using the good gifts God gave you? If it is still in the idea phase, does it present the possibility of great adventure? Has it been the thing lurking in your dreams for a long time? Do you suspect it will bear great fruit, great joy, great outcomes? Or maybe this: Are you just into it? That is reason enough.

I am a glass-half-full type by any measure. My hype people call it "refreshing enthusiasm," and my realists call it "naivety." Whatever. The following story exemplifies the type of yeses I've decided to embrace: Here in Texas, Brandon and I own an older house on a nearby lake. We bought it as an investment and mostly use it as rental property (five children + college = financial panic), but we also use it personally because all you have to do is put me by water and I transform into Your Best Friend, The Finest Mom, The Most Outstanding Christian, Your Favorite Lady. Whatever garbage I drive out to the lake with instantly evaporates when my eyeballs spy the water. All of a sudden I love everyone. I can handle life's dumpster fires. Marriage is easy. My children will all obviously succeed and flourish. The internet is a joy. Politics are about to get better.

Last year, I was on the upper boat deck with my best friends. We were irresponsibility sunning, because I will never forfeit my life theology, which is "tan fat is better than white fat." All of a sudden, we looked to our left, and A BEAUTIFUL YOUNG BRIDE AND GROOM were rowing toward us in a canoe, having just left their ceremony five houses down. We could hear the cheering. I stood straight up and screamed. Then I ran, nay, I *raced* inside and snatched a bottle of champagne from the fridge. As quick as my middle-aged legs could carry me, I dashed back outside and met them at the public dock next to our house, where they were tying up their adorable marital canoe. I handed them both glasses of cold, bubbly champagne and—please try to imagine this, dear reader—full-body hugged both of them in their gorgeous wedding clothes while wearing my old lady lake bathing suit. I gave them a brief (< lie) speech about marriage and love and gushed about what beautiful young things they were. We toasted with champagne, and I held her dress all the way back up to the road so she could return to the party after the most epic departure in the history of weddings. In classic Texan fashion, they invited me and my friends to their reception for "bull riding and beer." (You will never pry me out of this ridiculous state.) Here is my point:

I want to be a champagne runner.

This is my type of yes. Does this make sense? I am halfway through my life, beloveds. I am over the nonsense. I am for love. I am for encouragement. I am for grand gestures and over-the-top celebrations. I am for beauty and adventure and creativity. I am for you. I am for women. I am for the big, scandalous love of God for all us absurd humans. I am for taking myself less seriously. I am for second chances and extravagant gestures. I am for every person described as "a real character." I say yes to joy and risk. I say yes to inappropriate displays of affection. I say yes to cheering one another on. I say yes to letting the garbage go and embracing the good stuff. Life is simply too short to not say yes to these things. If I am lying on my death bed clutching decades of anger, regret, jealousy, and fear, I will be so, so sad.

Nanea Hoffman, CEO of Sweatpants and Coffee, wrote: "None of us are getting out of here alive, so please stop treating yourself like an afterthought. Eat the delicious food. Walk in the sunshine. Jump in the ocean. Say the truth that you're carrying in your heart like hidden treasure. Be silly. Be kind. Be weird. There's no time for anything else." Yes and amen! Dust off that *yes* stuck in your back pocket and put it into rotation. This is your one life. Get after it.

This brings us to the flip side of a Good Yes, which is a Necessary No. As the saying goes, the greatest enemy of the best is the good. Here is where our yeses need the nos as a solid partner. We can't add indefinitely. Each of us has a limited amount of time and energy, and it will reach its capacity. Choosing new yeses means a few new nos too. We subtract so we can add. Has something run its course? Has it outlived its usefulness or effectiveness? Has it lost its original joy? Is it simply neutral and thus a good candidate for subtraction in order to add elsewhere, even if what you "add" is more free time? Is there anything you can outsource? Can you relinquish control somewhere and hand off responsibility? Could you ask for assistance in order to create margin? Or does something just need to go because it needs to go? Some options simply deserve a "no" (my cousin Dori walked into our family reunion and told her kids, "You are not allowed to be attracted to anyone here").

I detect a lot of resentment in this space. Women are giving a ton of reluctant yeses, and they are mad and getting madder. "Most women have a difficult time saying no, especially if they think someone's feelings may be at stake or if they think they'll not be liked," wrote Dr. Kathryn Lively.

> Despite what most women think, this is not some immutable gene or biological defect. Rather, it is actually a socially learned coping mechanism that can, with a little time and attention, be unlearned. As young children, girls are socialized to be nice and to be more in touch with their own and other people's feelings than are boys. There's nothing wrong with being nice. And there is definitely nothing wrong with being liked . . . but there is something wrong when girls, and women, learn to subject their own needs to the point that they are taken advantage of or they end up doing things they don't want to do.[2]

Not only does this approach build up a reserve of bitterness, but we can only hide it for so long. It comes out sideways. When we refuse to say no to the detriment of our time, energy, or health, it will eventually make us furious at the person asking. This isn't even fair, because *we said yes* either overtly or with our silence. Again, ownership is critical here. You have agency over your choices. If you are saying yes when you want to say no, the only person who can reverse this is you. People can't read your mind. Nor do they necessarily know all the other responsibilities you carry. Most folks aren't trying to take advantage of you; they asked and you said yes, so this seems like the end of the transaction.

Let's discuss the problematic yeses you've already given. See if any of these admissions point to what's really inside your heart:

I said yes when I wanted to say no.
I said yes sincerely, but now life has shifted.
I said yes naively, and this isn't working.
I said yes because I felt bad.
I said yes because I felt obligated.
I said yes to spare someone's feelings.
I said yes gladly, but it has run its course.
I said yes, and now it is time to pass the reins.
I said yes, but I need to create margin now for something else.

We must be mature enough to own our own responses. While it may be true that someone else was manipulative or passive aggressive or irresponsible in their ask, if we said yes, then we said yes. A small but very current example: I fly out tomorrow morning for the first event on my spring tour, I am writing a book (Look! You are holding it! I did it!), I am in a blitzkrieg of podcast recordings, and I am doing some heavy lifting on the board of my church. I was supposed to launch my new book club last Friday with videos, emails, and all the enthusiasm it deserves. My development team has been working on it for three months. We were supposed to announce it at my tour events this week. Distraught, I texted my assistant Amanda the day before launch with a pathetic S.O.S.: "I JUST CAN'T DO IT. I NEED FOUR MORE WEEKS." Okay, honestly? I actually said, "I need one week," and my intuitive other brain Amanda insisted on four because she can only be the fall guy for my irresponsibility once.

Here is the truth: had I realistically looked at my calendar, my immovable responsibilities, and my writing deadline eight weeks ago when they proposed this date, I would have immediately known

I couldn't pull off a book club launch on Friday. Not only was all my time spoken for, but so was all my focus. Why did I agree to it? A combination of a debtor's mentality (when people work hard for me, I struggle to exert boundaries), an overestimation of my own capacity, an underestimation of the required time, and mental laziness—I didn't give the launch enough serious consideration when my team presented the date. It felt "later" at the time, so I carelessly pressed the yes button. So, rather than a smooth launch, I bailed on my team one day before our agreed-upon release and delayed the exciting project they'd been hustling on. This also meant they had to adjust expectations with our first author and her publisher. My sloppy yes caused a lot of problems, and rather than becoming a shining example of "all Jen can handle at once" like I imagined (this is the dark side of an Enneagram Three), it undermined my credibility, frustrated my team, and made me feel like a garbage person.

So, on the one hand, a heedless yes can cause a real mess for other people. On the other hand, it can create a perpetual mess for your own self. On their podcast *Dear Sugars*, Cheryl Strayed and Steve Almond interviewed Oprah on yeses and nos, and she exposed a bad no like this: "I did it. I only said yes so that person would think I was nice. But guess what? Two months later they were back asking again. They DID think I was nice so they asked for more! It worked for them!"[3] Why wouldn't someone believe the sincerity of our yes? If we gave it, they have the right to assume we meant it, so we might become human slot machines: just pull the lever and get more goodies! We all know women who feel incapable of denying requests, and they become ragged, exhausted helpers other people take advantage of with no reservations.

In Christian subculture, this conversation can get muddy. An absolute pillar of faith is serving each other, which, in genuine practice, is sometimes inconvenient, awkward, physically or emotionally taxing, and time-consuming. Of course it doesn't always dovetail neatly into our schedules or stop short of burdening. If "being hard" was an escape hatch for serving one another, this world would slip into despair. I want to be crystal clear that we are not exempt from being a good neighbor if it ever pinches. My community has carried me long past the moment it was easy, and I them. A life spent entirely on my own preferences would be utterly bankrupt. I don't believe in that worldview. The greatest depth of the human experience is inside meaningful relationships forged through loyalty, kindness, and compassion. We are all walking each other home. I've built a whole life on this truth (much more on this in chapter 10).

Again, I appeal to our common sense here. We need not check our hearts *or* our minds at the door. Reasonably, we can't reject every outside need presented to us and maintain any integrity, nor can we offer limitless energy and maintain our own health. These are binary arguments that don't have a useful bearing on grown women creating sustainable lives. If we can capture the "yes, but . . ." that creeps in here, trusting our good hearts and good intentions and good practices, we are free to move into a thoughtful assessment of our yeses and no's without shaming ourselves or each other.

In *Essentialism* (easily the best book I've read on this subject), Greg McKeown wrote,

> By applying tougher criteria we can tap into our brain's sophisticated search engine. If we search for "a good opportunity," then we will find scores of pages for us to think about and work through. Instead, we can conduct an advanced search and ask three questions: "What do I feel deeply inspired by?" and "What am I particularly talented at?" and "What meets a significant need in the world?" Naturally there won't be as many pages to view, but this is the point of the exercise. We aren't

looking for a plethora of good things to do. We are looking for our highest level of contribution: the right thing the right way at the right time.[4]

To help us as we consider our options, McKeown suggests the 90 percent rule, which looks like this: First, think about the single most important criteria for that decision. What is your goal? What endgame have you prioritized? What problem are you trying to solve? What is the main thing you are after? What are your nonnegotiables? How can your filter get as selective and specific as possible? Then, laser focused on that criteria, give each option a score from 0 to 100. If it scores below a 90, automatically change its rating to 0 and boot it.

This brilliant approach eliminates two key nonessentials: one, the enormous time and energy suck of indecision. Oh my word, I have lost *years* waffling back and forth, wringing my hands, talking myself into choices because I felt unclear or obligated. An 80 is a 0. The end. No emotional negotiations. This is so liberating. And, it saves you from getting stuck with a bunch of 60s or 75s. (As I wrote this paragraph, I texted Brandon and identified three 70s on my plate I need to purge.) You are clearing the deck for your 90s and above, which is where you will be most effective. Don't forget: this isn't just addressing a sense of overwhelm but applying a discipline to maximize your great gifts, not fragment them beyond usefulness. This application of tough criteria rescues us from impulsive, emotional decisions and forces us to use logic, reason, and intention.

Put another way, popular TED speaker Derek Sivers described his selective criteria like this: "If it's not a *hell yes*, it's a no." We put each choice to an extreme test: Do I feel wild with enthusiasm here? Does this require virtually no second-guessing? Does this line up with my convictions, talents, and service goals? Do I experience what Shonda Rhimes calls the hum: "When I am hard at work, when I am deep in it, there is no other feeling. The hum sounds like an open road and I could drive it forever. The hum is a drug, the hum is music, the hum is God's whisper right in my ear."[5] I love work like this—when time seems to evaporate and all cylinders are firing and creativity is sizzling. I know I've chosen a good yes, because I feel alive with energy. Also clear inside the hum: *I'm good at this*. Nothing better than running hard in your lane.

Certainly worth pointing out is that once these high-level decisions are made, next steps mainly look like old-fashioned work, so let's not slip into another fake argument that if life doesn't feel zippy at every moment, we get to eliminate the labor. This book, for example, was a HELL YES with no ambiguity. Am I enthusiastic and inspired by the content? Hell yes. Does this project line up with my giftings? Hell yes. Does this material meet a felt need in my community? Hell yes. An easy, all-in choice. A 95 rating.

But what followed the contract was an entire year and a half of serious labor. Writing on airplanes and in hotel rooms. Writing while everyone else was having fun. Endless conversations to hone the material. Sifting through thousands of pages of research. Cutting and reorganizing. Editing, and editing, and editing, and editing. Listening to the critiques of early readers, deciding which ones were dead to me, then adjusting the content even more. Arguing with my editor about which curse words I could keep. Participating in somewhere around a million conference calls about getting this book in your hands. More editing. At plenty of plot points, I felt less of a hum and more of a dead buzz, which I could only assume was the sound of the will to live draining out of my ear holes. Some marketing and PR makes me literally cry, so that bit turns me into Tim Burton's Corpse Bride. And then, of course, some very, very undiscerning readers won't like this masterpiece and they will say that on the World Wide Web, and other people will love the voyeurism and be like *Yay! Hate time!* and then I will announce I am becoming a bartender, which I will absolutely mean for at least three weeks.

I'm just saying that hell yeses still require work, which is sometimes full of "hum" and sometimes boring or hard. But still, inside the ecosystem of those deliberately chosen yeses, we come to life, serve the world well, feel the stretch and electricity of doing the thing we were made to do.

How do we say no gracefully so we can choose the right yeses? We get so hung up here. We pick the ease of five minutes of social compliance over the regret of a careless yes for days, weeks, months, or even years. It is ridiculous. I once said yes to a five-day "college tour" where I spent a hundred hours in the back of random cars driving to six itty-bitty colleges and speaking to rooms of *twelve* bored students. A whole week away from my family. I maybe addressed seventy-five late teenagers in total. The organizer was so earnest, so genuine, so not in possession of the average student's priorities on a Tuesday night. I said yes when I knew I should say no. To avoid this type of situation, McKeown made the following six suggestions (commentaries are mine):

1. *Separate the decision from the relationship.* Denying a request is not the same thing as denying the person. If I said yes every time my kids asked for something, they would all be millionaire teenagers with multiple cars, no curfews, an optional school schedule, and a poorly thought-out belly button ring.

2. *Learn how to say no gracefully, which sometimes doesn't mean using the word no.* I put this practice in play a few years ago. I am so polite, like, Jimmy Carter Deep South polite, and sounding rude is my nightmare. In regular rotation, my responses look like this: "Thank you so very much for this invitation. I deeply believe in your work and am grateful for your dedication

to it. Well done! Unfortunately, at this point, any new yes I give means a no to my family, so with sincere regret, I have to decline. Count on my support and prayers for your amazing event." I mean every word of this. I get invited to exactly zero terrible events. They are all good people doing good work with good intentions and good results. You can decline with graciousness and kindness.

3. *Focus on the trade-offs.* Rather than fixating on the loss of declining the offer, focus on the gain of what you get instead. When I politely decline an invitation to speak for the third time in the same week at a very, very worthy fundraiser, I get to be home on a Friday for pizza and movie night with my family. Cue: *Pretty in Pink* (we refuse to let our children grow up without a strong eighties indoctrination).

4. *Remind yourself that everyone is selling something.* I'm not being mean, but people are inviting you into their thing, and even if it is altogether good, they have a deal to sell in exchange for your time. If you don't automatically feel desperate to buy it, this could be a decent filter.

5. *Make your peace with the fact that saying no often requires trading popularity for respect.* While there may be a short-term impact on the relationship, research shows that once their initial annoyance or anger wears off, respect kicks in. People respect others with gracious but clear boundaries. It separates the pro from the amateur. I have experienced this virtually 100 percent of the time after giving a no. I once had an event planner email me a few weeks later: "Your kind no deeply affected me. I live in a world of unchecked, unmitigated yeses, and you gave me permission to say no with intention and grace."

6. *Remember that a clear no is more generous than a vague or non-committal yes.* The medium yes or maybe is the worst. Stringing people along or delaying the inevitable decline is a thousand

times worse than a polite but clear no on the front end. People know when they are getting a lukewarm placeholder. Further, they know when they are receiving wild, made-up excuses. We must stop doing this. We are fooling no one. It is actually better, easier, and more mature to say what you mean right out of the gate.[6]

Sisters, say yes when you mean yes and no when you mean no. Jesus had some killer counsel on this:

> And don't say anything you don't mean. This counsel is embedded deep in our traditions. You only make things worse when you lay down a smoke screen of pious talk, saying, "I'll pray for you," and never doing it, or saying, "God be with you," and not meaning it. *You don't make your words true by embellishing them with religious lace.* In making your speech sound more religious, it becomes less true. Just say "yes" and "no." When you manipulate words to get your own way, you go wrong. (Matthew 5:33–37 THE MESSAGE, emphasis added)

You don't make your words true by embellishing them with religious lace.
Or passive-aggressive lace.
Or conflict-avoidant lace.
Or martyrdom lace.
Or obligatory lace.

In making your speech sound more religious, it becomes less true.
In making your speech sound more agreeable, it becomes less true.

In making your speech sound more falsely enthusiastic, it becomes less true.

In making your speech sound more exaggerated, it becomes less true.

Just say yes or no.

On the one hand, you have the possibility of metaphorical Yes Trips, choices that shake you to life. The ones that say, "HERE I AM, WORLD. LET'S TANGO!" The ones that serve your best people with your best gifts. The ones that make this human life gorgeous, connected, renewed, that make you champagne runners to the world.

On the other hand, you have compassionate but necessary nos, the ones that clear space for your highest yeses, your 90s and above. Because guess what? Your 68 is someone else's 97. Let her have her spot! Clear her path! Don't take her space with your tepid 68 yes, because you are leaving 32 on the table that someone else could fulfill wholeheartedly. The world is equally, perfectly distributed. You have but one little note to play; you aren't Beyonce! Play your note! Leave the other chords to those who play them effortlessly. We are counting on your C minor, so bang that key with gusto.

WHAT I BELIEVE

9

I BELIEVE IN SPIRITUAL CURIOSITY

I walked into my first classroom a week before my twenty-second birthday. I was a new fourth-grade teacher in a competitive school district full of connected, veteran educators. Turnover was super low. (Who would leave?) I was the (severely) junior member on a team with two other teachers decades ahead of me, and we shared three classrooms of ten-year-olds. I knew nothing, I understood nothing, and I had no experience. I'm sorry, fourth graders from 1996 to 2000. I hope you went on to make something of yourselves. At least the rest of your education was above board.

Anyhow, one thing was sure: I loved the ornery boys. Always my favorites. I liked them a little wild, a little rotten, real stinkers but secretly adorable. The ones who would say the most inappropriate thing and make me burst out laughing despite my greatest attempt to be stern. My first favorite student was Ty, a scruffy, scrappy mess with huge dimples and an infectious grin (I tried to name *both* my son babies Ty and got vetoed). He'd wrap his arms all the way around me and squeeze as hard as he could anytime he acted up. It worked, let's see, about every single time. I loved him. He was the light in every room.

One day in the spring, Ty returned from my teammate's classroom, and all his sparkle was gone. I seated the kids with their books and took him into the hall. As I got my first good look at him, I noticed his face was blotchy and red, and he had some strange marks on his jaw.

"What happened?"

Ty fell into my arms sobbing. He'd mouthed off in my coteacher's room, class clown that he was, silly but harmless, and in a fit, she grabbed him by the cheeks and jaw and dragged him into the hall where she never let go, squeezing his face and soul into submission. Fifteen minutes later, I could still see the marks. As I stood there, holding this crying boy, my mind endured a brief but brutal fifteen seconds of panic.

What do I do? What am I supposed to do? What would our other partner do? Surely she didn't mean to hurt him? Did she mean to hurt him? Do I report my coteacher? Oh, my lord. I am twenty-two years old. She has been a teacher for fifteen years. What is going to happen if I report this? Will she get in trouble? What will the other teachers think? Is this disloyal? Am I overreacting? Should I ask her what happened? Should I let her explain? Should I have her back? Whose back should I have??

Drowning in confusion, I looked down at Ty's tear-stained face, swelling at the jaw, and I knew instantly. This was a breach of power, and no teacher should ever unleash her frustration on the body of a ten-year-old. This was not a spat between peers or even a heated argument between teacher and student. This was a person in power causing physical and emotional harm to a child in her care with no defenses. Adults are to be trust-worthy advocates for the children they are responsible for, and that included me.

I took him to my principal, bore witness to his story, and that was the last day I ever saw my coteacher. She was fired before the day's end and never came back to school.

With no language for power differentials and abuse back then, I still knew deep in my gut: sometimes you stand outside your team and do the right thing. If people in power maintain control at the expense of the vulnerable, if they exploit their authority and cause trauma, then even if I am a good-standing member of that domi-nant group, it is time to sound the alarm, come what may. I have to have the right backs.

I have been a religious insider my entire life. In my sliver of the pie chart, our denomination was led only by men, almost entirely white men, and it was predicated on a robust system of rules and consequences, morality and purity, authority and submission. Let me be absolutely fair: inside that ecosystem lived (and still live) some of the greatest people alive. Gifted teachers, faithful men and women, servants of the poor and disenfranchised, church mothers and fathers who raised me. But encapsulated in an institution, for me, the sum turned out to be less than its good parts. Systems have a way of corrupting even the purest intentions. Once the individual bright lights become dimmed sitting in committees, eclipsed by groupthink, and darkened with male power, the luster wears right off. Is this love? Is this God?

With the benefits of an adult brain, a broader range of experi-ences, and a departure from my echo chamber, I can say without question: my beliefs have been challenged. Everybody, relax. Katy, bar the door! A bit of good news: virtually every spiritual person has his or her beliefs challenged over a lifetime. Also good news: the Bible suggests this path is called *wisdom* and *maturity* and *growth* . . . not heresy and backsliding and unfaithfulness. Let's go ahead and take hyperbole out of this discussion.

A person asking hard questions of her faith system cares, and that means something. You are committed to mining the diamond out of the rubble, you stubborn thing. You believe in something good and just and loving, as Jesus insists he is, and you are determined to sift, to hang on. This doesn't indicate an anemic faith but the greatest kind. Like my beloved sister Sarah Bessey wrote in *Out of Sorts*: "Anyone who gets to the end of their life with the exact same beliefs and opinions as they had at the beginning is doing it wrong."[1]

"There's clearly a distinction between unhealthy and merely immature faith," wrote Harvey Edser. "Everyone on the spiritual journey has to go through the early stages of faith, just as everyone has to go through the early stages of human physical and psychological development. Immaturity isn't inherently unhealthy. It *becomes* unhealthy when an adult remains locked in immature patterns of thinking, behavior and relationship that belong to childhood; and the same applies in the spiritual life."[2]

My journey down this road of growth started with people, as it always does for me. I can identify the spiritual pain points in my own experience now, but as someone not prone to self-assessment, I saw it in others first. If faith is meant to produce new life, healing, great connection, flourishing, which *I believe*—I've built a whole life on this—I sure saw a lot of the opposite inside the structures. I noticed a great deal of shame pulled by the lever of fear. The rules were rigid and the consequences punitive. Gossip abounded, shrouded in "prayer requests," a thinly veiled way to talk trash about others' failures or choices, another clear signal to the group that missteps are catalogued and swift disapproval will make its rounds.

I saw the obviously gay kids laughing way too loud at the

anti-gay jokes by the youth pastor. I saw blood drain from the faces of girls as the True Love Waits teacher plucked the petals off a rose and held out a dead stick: "This is what you offer your husband when you give your petals away to your boyfriends." With horror, I recall the night in the youth group room we listed the "worst kids" in our high schools on a white board under the title *Bring 'em Back Alive*, drove to their houses, and *kidnapped* them back to church so they could meet Jesus: "Please don't be distracted by all your names on the board. We were just listing your sins publicly. Would you like to pray the Sinner's Prayer?"

Then, curiously, many of my peers left the church never to return. For something branded as abundant life, my version had thin staying power, very little abundance by any account. The threats of worldly destruction turned out to be false. The warnings of secular doom and empty marriages ruined by heavy petting were empty. After all that, our new classmates and coworkers didn't invite us to swinger parties or peddle heroin in the bathroom. The "world" we were taught to avoid (except during sanctioned moments of systematic evangelism) was filled with ordinary people who could be good and kind and wanted the same fulfilling life we thought we had the market cornered on.

As a thinking adult with permission to question systems, I finally asked: Where are the women? What about people of color? Tell me again why only men are in charge? Wait, so Catholics "aren't Christians," because why again? Why did so many leaders who fixated on our teen virginity end up in affairs, in sexual abuse scandals, covering up for one another? Can someone explain all these victims besides blaming their "obvious promiscuity" and kicking them out of their churches? Why is it Democrats are ruining the country? Explain how science is fake and the Bible is real? Why is Oprah a wolf in sheep's clothing again? Why couldn't we watch Scooby Doo? So the Southern Baptist Convention didn't offer a formal apology for its support of slavery and segregation until 1995? After 150 years of theological formation around the protection of white supremacy, are there any other interpretations that should be reexamined? Or was it just that one?

In the wake of all my questions, some of the beliefs I'd simply accepted for so long were challenged because, upon a more critical evaluation, they were the by-product of an obviously corrupt system, which has been historically dead last to the table of confession and repentance. Some of my beliefs were challenged because the same people were always in charge and we blithely hung pictures of White Jesus in our Sunday School rooms. Some of my beliefs were challenged because, while promising life abundant, they instead broke the hearts and trust of many outliers with a clear conscience.

Some of my beliefs were challenged because had I held to them as dictated, I would have no ministry, no authority, no agency over my own God-given gifts. Some of my beliefs were challenged because the missionary culture I grew up in often turned out to be a form of colonization. Some of my beliefs were challenged because they shamed girls and victims but protected men and abusers. Some of my beliefs were challenged because they too often failed to care for LGBTQ people and instead led to traumatic conversion therapy, forced celibacy, public humiliation, and ultimately suicide at seven times the normal rate. Some of my beliefs were challenged because they weren't producing many disciples, mostly just gatekeepers and defectors. Some of them felt bad in my soul, damaging in my practices, harmful to my brothers and sisters, a betrayal of the Spirit of God.

Let's talk about you. Having led women for years, I know we do not all come to this discussion from the same background. We have every kind of Christian, semi-Christian, recovering Christian, and non-Christian in this community. Some of us grew up under the steeples. Some of us went twice a year. Some of us didn't think about faith or Jesus until adulthood. Some of us are shocked to even still be reading this chapter because faith seems like a placebo pill for dumb-dumbs. Fine. Good. All are welcome. I think of faith in such broad strokes these days. I'm super into Jesus, which I'll talk more about in a minute, but a bunch of the trappings we've built around him are rubbish. It's okay to say this.

"The only way to understand what is currently happening to us as 21st-century Christians in North America is first to understand that about every 500 years the church feels compelled to hold a giant rummage sale," wrote Phyllis Tickle in *The Great Emergence*. "About every five hundred years, the empowered structures of institutionalized Christianity, whatever they may be at that time, become an intolerable carapace that must be shattered in order that renewal and new growth may occur."[3]

The last "garage sale" occurred in the sixteenth century with the Great Reformation; five hundred years before that was the Great Schism; and five hundred years prior to that takes us to the sixth century to the fall of the Roman Empire and the coming of the Dark Ages. Each time the story is broken, a new imagination emerges and faith spreads in dramatic ways.

Although I don't specialize in math, according to Tickle's thesis, we are again at the five-hundred-year mark, thus many of the tectonic shifts and fractures within two seemingly totally different versions of western Christianity make perfect sense. I see it in evangelicalism for sure, but the Vatican II suggests similar rumblings inside Catholicism, and the rise of women's authority in the global charismatic and house church movements suggest the same.

My point is this: we are not the first culture or generation to push hard on the spiritual forms of our faith system. Don't be afraid. We are not capable of rendering Jesus extinct. I believe he is going to make it. We are one tiny speck in a great constellation of People Trying to Figure Out God Throughout History. A tiny speck. (A faithful synagogue attender from two thousand years ago would be gobsmacked in any one of our churches today.) Faith is reliably resilient, meandering from generation to culture to country to century, adjusting its packaging but somehow retaining its core.

So we'll start here: if you have some spiritual questions, if something you were taught rings hollow in adulthood, if you are even considering another perspective or interpretation or experience, you can join the ranks of every serious Christian before you. You are in good company. Don't be shamed out of your search. Questions have historically scared the establishment, because they threaten power structures. More generously, most folks within the system just want to be faithful, and when someone challenges the tenets, it holds the possibility we were wrong or maybe just limited, and certainty is one of the only things we control.

Having sorted through the Bible and all its teachings, it feels disorienting when someone else pushes hard on our conclusions. We are not naturally good at this space. Maturity would stay open and curious, but we are fragile, scared, weird little humans who struggle enough, and can't we all just agree on one damn thing already?

Also worth noting is whether your questions involve the structures (so important and worth asking) or interpretations (same). Are your questions about church policy and systems? Or about theology and Jesus? These obviously cross over, as theology informs structures (only men are in charge in certain branches, because they believe that is biblical), but sometimes you can parse out your questions by isolating them for scrutiny.

Systematically, no person of integrity could ever suggest one limb of the tree has it exactly right. That is patently absurd. There are more than nine thousand Protestant denominations alone. There are variations on every single practice, every single liturgy, every single interpretation, every single organizing principle, every single spiritual expression, every single leadership structure. Of course, most key leaders in any sect will point to the Bible as their handbook, finding supporting evidence for their practices. This is easily done. Some of the Bible is weird, and all of it was located in an ancient, Middle Eastern context. And once a particular group assigns modern meaning to any section and teaches it thusly, it becomes surprisingly hard to imagine it differently. You come to believe that Saint Paul had something meaningful to say about using a drum kit in the Sunday service.

So, in terms of organizing church principles, I hold almost everything loosely. Choirs, bands, one-hour services, four-hour services (black friends, I love you, but I am hungry and ready for lunch), liturgy, communion—all of this is up for grabs. These are matters of preferences; there is no right and wrong. If you find God in high church, sister, light the candles and dial into the lectionary. If you worship best with a demonstrative Hillsong band and a pastor in ripped jeans, get after it. If you need a little, bitty country church composed of grandmas and traditions, that place awaits.

What I do not hold loosely: Is this church a place of spiritual flourishing? Is it brimming with Good News? Is everyone welcome to participate, serve, and lead? Does this organization leave a whole group out by its policies? Would someone experience harm here by virtue of polity? Is this church wildly obsessed with Jesus? If every human being is not safe in its seats—protected, cherished, respected, able to contribute—then that church breeds death, not life. I don't care how pretty or polished or popular it is. Just ask anyone who has suffered under that type of administration. But if the possibility for all human flourishing exists, if the table of Jesus is wide and open to all, if the leadership is marked by humility, I suggest you grab on to that band of ragamuffins and hold on for dear life.

The church has been the source of my greatest sorrow and

greatest joy. On some Sundays in our ratchet little church in South Austin, I look around at those weirdos from every walk of life, serving this city with gladness, loving each other in the messiest way, and I just cry. Brandon and I started our church in 2008, and it remains one of the greatest loves of my life. I could write a thousand pages on how we've failed and changed and repaired. So don't hear me say a good church is one that never hurts you, never gets it wrong, never catastrophically blunders. I don't believe that church exists. The question is, what do they do with the pain they cause? Own it, apologize, fix it, turn from it? If your church knows what to do with failure, you may never do better.

Your questions might have to do with theology, the actual stuff of belief. Again, you join the ranks of a great host of witnesses who have pressed hard on the Scriptures for millennia. In this sometimes anxiety-provoking work, I commend your faithfulness. Bewildered Christians often suggest that wrestling with theology indicates weakness and disobedience, but, beloved, this is simply not true. I reject this accusation for you, for me, for the church. Your questions mean nothing of the sort; they signal a heart after truth. Anytime Brandon and I have reexamined a principle, we wrestled through Scripture, not around it, ever convinced that in Jesus was life and if all we saw was death around a specific interpretation, perhaps we owed it to the Bible to dig further into it.

"The Bible is clear," is the thing people say around complicated subjects—an effective end to any discussion, a shield against tension points where our interpretations are either causing obvious harm or challenging the prevailing opinion. The truth is, the Bible is not a handbook or a church manual or a list of rules. It has taken my entire life to understand this.

"Christians and Jews have always been 'reimagining' God—adapting the sacred past of their tradition to discern God's presence here and now," wrote Pete Enns in *How the Bible Actually Works*.

That process of adapting the past is also baked directly into the Christian Bible itself, Old and New Testaments. The biblical authors accepted their sacred responsibility to *employ wisdom when engaging their sacred tradition.* As should we—always respectful of the past, but never assuming that we are meant to recreate it and live in it; always tied to this ancient tradition, but without expecting it to do the heavy lifting for us. . . . We are always processing God and faith not from a high place free of our entanglements, but from the vantage point of our inescapable humanity—our reason, experience, tradition, and scripture.[4]

Learning to discern what is eternal and what is simply a product of our own context is actually harder work than accepting any interpretation on its face. It removes the comfort of certainty, which can admittedly make our chests feel tight. If religion has ever agreed on anything, it is each generation's certainty of their certainty. Dissenters are rarely appreciated until they are dead and their voices from the margins turned out to be true.

History treats kindly the courage of Jesus, Abraham Lincoln, Ghandi, Medgar Evers, Martin Luther King, Jr., Harvey Milk, and, to a general degree, the millions of women who contested the patriarchy, but their own communities and contemporaries killed them for it. If you object to linking civic challengers with biblical challengers, please remember the Bible has been used to justify human rights abuses since its canonization, including every injustice these freedom fighters opposed. It was "right" until it clearly wasn't. Hindsight is clear on the arc of moral justice, but the present day is not.

In my experience, women are *riddled* with spiritual questions and normal theological shifts but are too scared to be honest. The threat of excommunication, family outrage, community rejection, and even the genuine fear of being wrong keeps many women silent. This is definitely one of the mismatches between our inside convictions and outside declarations.

I want to acknowledge this concern as legitimate. Closing this breach *does* include the possibility of turmoil. I have great empathy for this space and hold your process in high regard. I counted the same costs and paid them, and they were high. This is real. When you reimagine a belief, an interpretation, when you consider a different church or entire denomination, if you demonstrate curiosity toward a new hermeneutic or body of biblical scholarship, this creates ripples in the spiritual life you've already built. I understand the compulsion to bury your questions and stay silent.

I also affirm the very disorienting, slightly scary internal feeling spiritual de- and reconstruction creates. It is strange to be at odds with the scaffolding that once held up your faith, even if only one part of it. It's lonely. If you are accustomed to following rules like I was, a good Christian soldier, asking new questions seems rebellious and defiant, and your own voice will pile on to the kickback. This is normal, and I'm sorry. I wish spiritual curiosity was celebrated in our community like in the Jewish tradition.

As my dear friend Rachel Held Evans, now passed, wrote in *Inspired*,

> For Jewish readers, the tensions and questions produced by Scripture aren't obstacles to be avoided, but rather opportunities for engagement, invitations to join in the Great Conversation between God and God's people that has been going on for centuries and to which everyone is invited. . . . While Christians tend to turn to Scripture to *end* a conversation, Jews turn to Scripture to *start* a conversation.[5]

Alas, our spiritual culture operates in absolutes, so natural curiosity is viewed with hostility. Thus it is perfectly reasonable that favoring hard questions over easy answers leaves you feeling adrift. All I have to offer you is my experience, but this is as plain as I can say it: although there is loss built into this process, I wouldn't go back to secret tension for all the public approval in the world. I cannot adequately explain the liberation in addressing your questions and owning your own convictions. *I am free.* No more hiding, no more back-room conversations with only safe people, no more fear. I'm on the other side of the hard part, and it was all worth it.

Our life has become so expansive—full of new people and wide ideas and a fresh movement of God. There is a whole world out here I didn't know about, and it is changing my life. It is marked by kindness and curiosity, and it insists that the Good News is supposed to be good. If I used to be popular but deeply troubled on the inside, now I am less popular but wild with holy fire in and out. It all matches, and I would not undo one solitary second of the last few years.

This will sound redundant at this point in this book, but you have permission to speak honestly. You get to ask hard questions of faith. You are allowed to reexamine something you were taught. A serious person of faith is willing to evolve. First-century Jewish rabbis would be shocked how this searching process has devolved from a cornerstone of development to cause for alarm. Jesus told that interesting story about wineskins for a reason. This story has been a source of comfort to me for a decade.

It goes like this: Before we got civilized and put our wine in bottles, God made people use animal skins for wine storage, I'm pretty sure just to get this one story out of Jesus. So a freshly [checks notes] shorn sheep skin was fashioned into a bag for wine. Why did the ancients house their Cabernet inside dead animal flesh? I don't make the rules. I told you the Bible could be weird. Freshly pressed wine could only be poured into brand-new skins, because, as fermentation developed and the wine expanded, new wine skins could stretch with the process. They had a lot of give, not a lot of wear. Over time, though, after skins had been used for loads of parties and weddings and feasts and Tuesday nights, they would become brittle and stretched to capacity.

Thus, Jesus explained, "No one puts new wine into old wineskins. For the old skins would burst from the pressure, spilling the wine and ruining the skins. New wine is stored in new wineskins so that both are preserved" (Matthew 9:17 NLT). In other words, containers run their course. They hold the goods as long as they can, but after a season, they have stretched as far as they can go, they've become brittle, and the inevitable outcome of continuing to use them as holders is that *everything gets destroyed*—the delicious wine and the container. It's all a mess on the floor and Tuesday night is ruined.

Dear one, the wine is still good. If you are asking hard questions, it is because you love the wine. You believe it is good and marvelous and worthy of consumption. It has real lasting power. The wine has managed to woo every generation since time began. You are asking questions of the wineskins, which is wise and appropriate, because *they don't last*. They stretch as long as they can, but at some point, they have to be replaced so the wine can keep flowing.

New ideas, new understanding, new forms, new perspectives—don't miss the result of these courageous expansions: "both are preserved." You are not rejecting the wine but simply noticing the brittle places where the pressure is untenable, and, in choosing new wineskins, you save the whole enterprise. So many women tell me they've rejected the wine, but upon further examination, they just stuck with an old wineskin too long. It can be hard to distinguish between a burst container and the wine it spilled when it is lying in ruins together on the floor.

I contend the wine is still as worthy as ever.

Jesus is good. He is love and love alone. He is for us, never against us. He fixed the broken space between us and God. He was the greatest living human (he slayed at humanity) and lives to intercede eternally for us still. I believe that in him is life. I'll never believe anything else, anything less. He doesn't subscribe to our human hierarchies and systems of power, no matter what powerful people say. Jesus loved women and children and sick people and, irrationally, Roman leaders oppressing his people. No one could tell Jesus crap about who he was supposed to honor and dishonor. His grace knew no bounds, which people loved and hated and ultimately killed him for, but Jesus didn't care because he just came back alive and saved the world.

He is in the saving business. Don't let anyone tell you differently.

Let's go back to the potential objections to your process, the hard conversations around your spiritual movement. First, you are a learner, not a seminary professor, so it is not your responsibility to perfectly articulate your journey to someone else. This is a stubborn obstacle for women. *How will I explain this? I don't know if I can get the words right.* You don't have to. Early stages of spiritual examinations are often muddy and difficult to summarize. This doesn't mean you are dumb. It means you are doing the laborious work of deconstructing and reconstructing and listening and learning and praying about all this, and, excuse me, but this is not the best time to explain yourself to Aunt Margaret. If Aunt Margaret is sincerely interested in what you are exploring, she can do her own work.

This may have surprising consequences. When Brandon and I embraced affirming LGBTQ theology after two years of careful examination (sometimes it takes that long to replace old hardwiring), his mom had "some concerns" and listened intently, as she had the same question and was actually hungry for relevant resources. (Jacki is a lifelong conservative and faithful Christian; never make assumptions about someone else's faith. We cannot possibly know how God is challenging another person in the quiet of his or her own soul.) Brandon gave her every book we read (supporting both arguments) and a complete list of resources we consulted. *She read every single one.* Rather than clamp down in fear, Jacki did her own heavy lifting and then some. Her sincere investigation took her to the world of sexual and biological science, which has come light years in decades, and this clinched it for her. (I checked this paragraph with her, and I wish I could insert her entire response. This sentence was particularly classic Jacki: "I read all the studies and responses on clinical evidence supporting genome and epigenome genetic links completed recently." LOL. She is a real science type. And then this beauty: "Original texts in the original languages do not say what we're reading and interpreting within our context in our culture. God's word is inerrant, but man is not.") The whole six-month operation spit her out on the other side fully affirming.

Her process will go down as one of the greatest examples of spiritual maturity I've witnessed in my life.

This was not the case across the board, as you might imagine, nor will it be for you, whatever interpretation or structure you are examining. While you are not responsible to do the heavy lifting for your community, here are some responses that might aid you in conversation or conflict:

Would you like a list of resources I am learning from?

I'm still working out how to understand this.

I am asking questions. I don't have all the answers.

Have you ever had any questions about this?

I appreciate your concern. I understand how change feels.

Tell me more about your unease.

Have you ever evolved in a belief or interpretation?

Have your thoughts on church structures ever evolved?

I am approaching this with great care, not carelessness.

I believe the best of your intentions. Please believe the best of mine.

I am the same person you love.

Let's walk this out to its furthest possible conclusion. What are you scared of?

Thank you for talking openly with me. I have a different conviction.

We can come to different conclusions here and still love each other.

Just as it is not your responsibility to explain your every step, it is also not your job to change someone's mind. You get to be a thinking, reasonable, discerning woman who takes her faith seriously. Full stop. Your convictions do not come with a built-in requirement for arguing or convincing, no matter how much you are baited. You do not have to attend every fight you are invited to.

Nor do you have to defend yourself. Depending on how deeply you are embedded in a specific faith community, there may even be a feeding frenzy, one of our worst characteristics. If your niche is particularly uncharitable, you may be called names, shamed, rebuked, iced out. Listen to me: you will not die of conflict, resolved or not. It will not kill you, dear one. You will live. They will live. The church will live. You can handle this. Conflict may seem like the worst deterrent imaginable, but it is worse still to suffocate your convictions in favor of approval. That will eat you alive.

Here is my best advice: keep living. Keep being the same person you've been. Keep doing the good and kind things you've always done. Keep loving Jesus. Keep pressing hard on your faith; I hope we are doing this until we are dead. Keep being kind. Keep serving. Asking new questions isn't the spiritual catastrophe you've been told. The slippery-slope argument is lazy, as if you are a spineless sheep incapable of higher-level thinking and discernment. You are a grown woman. Stand on your own two feet.

I have some good news. There is a whole wonderful world outside. You are not alone, no matter how crazy others make you sound. Millions of faithful people have asked new questions of faith and systems, and guess what? They still love God! They are serving despite religious disapproval. They are good brothers and sisters who, against all odds, still sometimes love the church, and that is primarily because they *are* the church.

And a final word to my readers still spiritually thriving inside the traditional system: I could not possibly be happier for you, and that is sincere. Those forms can be life-giving, and, as I mentioned earlier, some of the finest people on earth serve there. I learned to love Jesus inside those structures, and look at me . . . it sure stuck. If each iteration of the church raises the next generation to take the baton, even if they run their leg a little differently, we have to be grateful for their legacy. I am regularly mentored by a few leaders whose entire operation is in the bullseye of traditional church. They are dear brothers and sisters, and I can attest to their undisputed faithfulness. "They" are not "all" anything.

Furthermore, spiritual exploration is nurtured in plenty of conventional spaces. No type of church is a monolith, and we would be liars to suggest the steeples are all stale and the only freedom is out in the wilderness. If your traditional faith community is a place of great human flourishing, if you increasingly love God and people more, I celebrate it. We are all just taking various roads to the same home.

Wherever you ask them, you will not regret letting your inside spiritual questions and, ultimately, their conclusions live on the outside of your life. Especially if your tension points involve theological issues that oppress others. When you are ninety-five years old on your death bed (I am very optimistic about your life span), you will be so proud of any hard spiritual work you engaged in to roll out freedom for more people, even if that means yourself. *Have the right backs.* I am convinced that maturing faith doesn't get smaller and tighter but wider and freer. As our psychological development moves from a tightly controlled childhood environment with rules and restrictions toward an adulthood governed by discernment and understanding, so goes our spiritual development.

In whatever faith community we've chosen, our questions should evolve. We no longer ask: What are the rules? What is the line? Who is in and who is out? Who is right and who is wrong? What do we do with dissenters? What is allowed? How do we maintain *what is*? Wonderfully, we begin to ask instead: Where is the life? What does a flourishing faith system look like? What feels and sounds and looks like actual good news? Where is there more joy and less fear? What is kind? What is generous? What feels like Jesus? Where are people coming back to life, coming back to God?

This is good work, sisters. I honor your commitment to the better questions. May you courageously ask them, diligently seek the answers, then help build the church we want to pass on to our children. A flourishing world awaits.

10

I BELIEVE IN THIS CAUSE

I t is my great fortune to have five children, because it is their mission in life to help me know things. Where would I be if my nondrivers weren't giving me driving instructions from the back seat? I guess off in a ditch or blowing through every stop sign in the greater Austin area. They deeply understand vehicular management, and, lucky for me, they are here to help. Furthermore, they have sage advice on how to discipline their siblings, which is useful, because I'm just a silly lady out of my depth in serious need of parenting suggestions from fourteen-year-olds. I also deeply appreciate their financial planning guidance, because, as it turns out, they have well-reasoned ideas on how we should spend our money. What's that? This $45,000 car is a sound investment for a junior in high school because it retains its value? Thank you for helping me understand the marketplace. Now I know an important thing.

Additionally, my children educate Brandon and me on the lifestyles of their peers, because evidently we are way beyond the pale and they believe we should know. For example, all their friends have an iPhone 10. Every one of them. We had no idea! Our poor Oliver Twists have to make do with passed-down phones, because, when we have an available upgrade, the people who get the new phones are named Brandon and Jen Hatmaker, and the reason is because we pay for the phones with the money we earn from our jobs. Good to know that all the other parents, I'm guessing, still use landlines so their eighth graders can take better selfies with their thousand dollar phones. Noted. Also noted is that none, exactly zero of their friends, have bedtimes or curfews. This is so interesting! We didn't realize. Here we are, like officers in a detention camp, making our children, nay, our *hostages*, go to bed on school nights. This is remarkably unfair, and our spawn have helped us understand that.

Finally, they are key reporters in the various ways other adults conspire against their basic success. For example, our son's football coach deliberately overthrew passes to him, so he'd look bad enough at practice to not make the A Team. It was an obvious conspiracy to favor his preferred players; everyone knows this. HOW DARE HE? Additionally, one of our sons actually earned a C, but his teacher "made him" get a D. She did this. Here I thought teachers were educating the next generation, but apparently they are just out here failing children willy nilly, *children who did nothing wrong.* Someone should alert the authorities.

Recently, one of my kids explained the FDA's attack on imported cheeses containing "cheese mites" as "another example of government overreach, Mom!" What is the bleak future of artisanal cheeses in North America? I mean, are we just going to let the Deep State mandate our cheese options? Is this the life we want for our children and grandchildren? So, I helpfully responded: "LET'S ORGANIZE A MARCH."

The child was deeply aggravated by what appeared to be a

sarcastic reaction to this authoritarian threat, but I was just suggesting a great tool for activists against unjust regulations on our snacks.

I am relatively new to the world of marches. My first was the MLK March here in Austin six years ago. I've since laced up my shoes for many, like the Women's March, Pride, March for Our Lives, all so impossibly exciting, I can't believe it took me so long. Coming together in peaceful solidarity with thousands of like-minded people in support of human rights and civic change is absolutely inspiring. I cry every time.

I may be newish to marches, but I am not new to the work of justice. Not every social issue has a corresponding march, of course, but the metaphor stands: for the things that move us most, we are willing to take to the streets. There comes a point when we move from *I would stand by you* to *I would march for you*. Not only will I quietly lend support from the sidelines, but I will take up the banner.

My radar is so sensitive to injustice, I can smell it in the air a mile away. This has been a long road in the same direction. Early on, this was nothing but instinct, as my personal experience was homogeneously privileged in every way. I *felt* injustice so deeply I would lose sleep, but I had no language or history or conceptual knowledge of systemic inequity. Forgive the woo-woo suspicion, but I believe God had plans for me of which justice work was central, and none of that is possible without a strong compass toward equality. Thus, a white girl in white Kansas in a white Southern Baptist church with no immigrant, gay, or neighbors of color would eventually find herself marching for all these friends. God finds a way to do what he wants with us, man.

I can't understand a world without advocacy, defined as "to support or argue for (a cause, policy, etc.): to plead in favor of."[1] I am my sister's keeper for damn sure. If we stop pleading in favor of each other, of justice, of equality, of shalom on this shaky earth, we are doomed. The notion of *every man for himself* is so radically destructive. The suggestion that personal or national sovereignty reigns supreme is the antithesis to the "kingdom of Jesus," which, if unfamiliar, is the one where the last is first, the least the greatest, our neighbors like flesh and blood, our enemies—spoiler alert—also our neighbors. Jesus said the kingdom of God belongs to children, if that helps clear it up. This is the citizenship you want, trust me. In this magical place, no one would suffer alone, systems wouldn't oppress, every single person would be valued equally. Whatever weirdness Christians have afflicted upon culture, Jesus was the straight-up real deal. Go back to the source material if you need to become recentered.

Advocacy has a learning curve, and I would call it steep. On its face, it appears simple if you are in my demographic. White Saviorhood is low-hanging fruit for . . . well-meaning but ill-informed do-gooder types (the title of my next book; a memoir). We shall come to your poor/uneducated/primitive neighborhood/community/nation, and we shall bring our evangelicalism/Vacation Bible Schools/ignorance and we shall poorly paint your church/bypass your own leadership/unknowingly condescend and we shall take many pictures/never come back/feel bad about you but good about ourselves. I HAVE DONE THIS. Brandon and I chaperoned masses of teenagers to inflict no good whatsoever on communities that secretly didn't appreciate our unskilled construction. Turns out, people aren't dumb, helpless, or incapable. American Christians do not actually know what is best for the rest of the world. I'm not making this up. This is the intel from The Rest of the World.

Closer in, I've learned the key difference between making myself the main character in the story of oppressed people as a "woke advocate" (nope) and actually sitting at their feet as a learner, their voices in the microphone, not mine. There is no such thing as "I am a voice for the voiceless" . . . people actually have voices! Whole voices! The question is, who has the microphone? As a straight white lady with a ton of unearned privilege, I am best qualified as an Aaron, not a Moses; I can hold up the arms of the actual prophets leading their people out of bondage, not take their place. (My early advocacy for racial equality was so cringey, I WANT IT STRICKEN FROM THE RECORD, INTERNET.)

I often made the mistake of starting in the middle of engaging an issue, well-intentioned but dumb as a sack of diapers. Urgency can convince us to skip the pesky steps of listening, learning, and processing. Since I burn pretty hot, I get why outrage or sorrow can shoot us out of the starting blocks without warming up. We see something wrong and want to help make it right. This instinct is noble, literally how we were created to thrive.

We are wired to care about what other people want and need. As socially influenced individuals, sharing the values and concerns of our neighbors creates social harmony. Embedded in our psyches is the sense that, when our neighbors are suffering, the whole community is at risk. We instinctively know what we should all be experiencing: justice, equality, safety, agency, belonging, and we are highly tuned to these goals for each other. It is why injustice cuts most of us so deeply.

In a recent study at Princeton, researchers found when mothers looked at pictures of their babies, the same region in their brains lit up as when they imagined harm being done to others. Their own children and victims of violence—two very different subjects, yet united by a similar neurological reaction. This suggests that compassion isn't just a fickle emotion but an innate response embedded in our brains. In short: *we are designed to mother each other through pain.*

In similar research out of Emory University, participants were given the chance to help someone while their brain activity was recorded. Helping others triggered portions of the brain that also turn on when people receive rewards or experience pleasure. This is remarkable: helping others brings the same exact pleasure as personal gratification.

Not only do our brains reward us for compassionate behavior, the rest of our body does too. For example, when we feel threatened, our automatic nervous system (ANS) kicks in, and our heart and breathing rates usually increase, preparing us for the "fight or flight" response. What is the ANS profile of compassion? As it turns out, when adults feel compassion for others, this emotion also creates very real physiological changes: their heart rates go down from baseline levels, which prepares them not to fight or flee but to approach and sooth. Additionally, nurturing behavior floods our bodies with oxytocin, a chemical reaction in the body that motivates us to be even *more* compassionate,[2] an internal prize for kindness.

Thank you for coming to my neuroscience class.

We are meant for this, you guys! We are made to love each other!

This is why we go all bull-in-a-china-shop sometimes. We are designed to feel the emotions of one another, so the pain of others triggers something primal in us. But rather than jumping in uninformed, grabbing the steering wheel when we should be in the passenger seat, advocacy requires a stage of listening and learning. No matter how wild with passion you are over an issue or people group or need, someone else is already on the ground with more knowledge, experience, and best practices. Someone else is already on the ground having long been on the receiving end of that injustice. Someone else is already on the ground with hard-won lessons, a mobilized community, and an accurate perception of the big picture. Helping poorly can be worse than not helping at all.

The best advocates are humble about learning. My dear friend

Latasha Morrison founded a nonprofit called Be the Bridge as a vehicle for racial healing in the church and culture. Her work equips bridge builders toward developing vision and skills for racial unity. Her space is full of white folks shielded from the lingering effects of white supremacy embedded in minds, perceptions, and systems and thus mostly unaware of its ramifications. Latasha developed many educational resources, including a multiracial private Facebook group for interested people. She created a rule for new members, which is carefully moderated to keep the space safe: "You don't get to post your own or make a comment on anyone else's post for *three months*."

She requires ninety days of humble listening, because the first response from most white people at the beginning of their learning curve is defensiveness, which translates to offensiveness. It's another way we tend to make things about us in a story that belongs to people of color. Latasha is not harsh; she is a leader protecting the space from racial harm, unintended or not. As a student of hers, this approach changed my life. I listened exclusively for almost a year, and it took every single day of that to lock in. What seemed confusing or downright baffling in month one felt crystal clear after learning for a solid year. I didn't know what I didn't know, and that online space was my classroom and the community my teachers.

What do you care about? What keeps you up at night? Who can you not stop thinking about? Our bodies sometimes tell us what matters to us. Where are your emotions outsized? Where are your strong feelings located? What triggers you, even if your reaction surprises you? Where does your heart keep looking? Whose faces do you see in your mind's eye? (This is how my family moved into adoption. I was not a person who always knew I'd adopt. It never crossed my mind until it did, and then it wouldn't leave my mind. It was my singular thought until Ben and Remy were in my arms.

Adoption is a perfect example of how your heart may lead you in, but your mind must immediately take over and do a ton of research, because this is maybe the worst possible arena to be armed with nothing but good intentions.)

The good news is that you can care about what you care about, and I can do the same, and between us all, everything is covered. What would I march for metaphorically? The eradication of white supremacy, LGBTQ rights and dignity, gun reform, women's safety and equality worldwide, a safe family for every child, the end of human trafficking. What would you march for? Care of the earth, campaign reform, animal rescue, equality in education, media literacy, healthcare rights, religious freedom, criminal justice reform, more libraries, reforestation, care of veterans, early childhood intervention, maternal health, prison ministry, the return of cursive instruction in elementary schools, FDA reversal on cheese mite regulations, anything! Put it in the bucket! Look at all the things we can plead in favor of!

Put yourself under the leadership of the greatest people and organizations you can find in the space. Read and study and listen and learn. Volunteer behind the scenes, if that makes sense in your field. An invaluable tool of mine is studying the critiques. What do the critics of this advocacy say? Where are the tension points? What do the front lines look like out there? What conversations are like-minded advocates having right now? If your conviction is related to injustice for a group of people, your very first stop is pulling up a chair to their table and learning from their experiences. Remember, no one is actually voiceless. People have voices, just not enough listeners. There is no substitute for the lived experience of the people you care about. Do your homework. Log your time. Develop your understanding. Learn from the right leaders. Take it seriously.

Then get after it.

If ever there was a moment to make sure our internal convictions were living loud and proud on the outside, it is in advocacy. Our sincere concern is useless lying dormant inside our minds. Here is where the rubber can leave the road, because compassion work takes time, energy, and sometimes courage. It is fashionable to be an Internet Advocate where Woke Words generate a lot of buzz without the grind of any actual work. To be fair, words are quite powerful when challenging systems of injustice—we need them and they matter—but we also have to put our boots on the ground. Eventually, we must champion our cause out loud in word and deed.

Let's talk about that courage bit. Most advocacy challenges unjust systems, and they all have gatekeepers around their preservation. There is a power dynamic in every biased system. People do not suffer unfairly in a vacuum but at the hands of corruption, greed, prejudice, and the status quo. If someone is kept on bottom, someone else remains safely on top. These systems are confusingly defended, particularly if they have a partisan reputation. You will discover people arguing against their own best interests, or their children's best interests, because an issue is part of a bundle they've been conditioned to resist or defend. It is maddening but also daunting.

Thus, courage is required for advocacy, because criticism is guaranteed.

A couple of months ago, I got a call from the middle school counselor. She put my daughter on the phone, and it took me three minutes to understand what she was saying through her sobs and wails. Between gasps, she told me that another student said she would be deported because she was "an illegal" born in Ethiopia, and America is getting rid of them now. Only thirteen and not in possession of international adoption policy, this made perfect sense to my daughter, as several of her Mexican classmates or members of their families had been deported. I sped to school in half the normal time and took her straight home. It took two hours to convince her that she was a legal, permanent citizen. I had to lay out all our social security cards and legal documents and put our adoption lawyer on the phone.

Once she fell into a sweaty, exhausted sleep, I was back at school with my hair on fire. We are our children's first and best advocates; I learned this from my dad who never met one of my enemies who wasn't his enemy and a clear enemy of the Lord Almighty. Regret from the school administration over this insidious form of targeted bullying wasn't enough. I needed to hear next steps, assurance of meaningful discipline, a discussion on prevention in a school where minority students compose 60 percent of the population. I have the longest imaginable fuse for my own critics, but you mess with one of my kids, you unleash racism on their young souls, and I turn into the Incredible Hulkess.

This advocacy was met with great compassion, because this type of traumatic terror is unthinkable for "one of ours" (until adulthood, she gets the built-in protective covering of my whiteness). But although there is not a single meaningful difference between a thirteen-year-old child forced apart from her mother at a port of entry and my thirteen-year-old child who thought she might be, when I raised money to reunite immigrating families forcibly separated at the border, my feed was jammed with outrage:

> "Let them all live with you, and then we'll see how much
> you care!"
> "They should have stayed in their own country!"
> "Finally, some tough measures at the border!"

Be prepared: a ton of advocacy work will draw criticism. We live in a diverse world with conflicting ideas about how to govern it, steward it, serve it, and live in it. Our experiences create varied wells of compassion. Our environments shaped our perceptions and politics and passions. We hold different worldviews. One person believes a system needs to be shored up, and another believes it should be dismantled top to bottom, so I've learned to stay focused on who and what I am advocating for and far less on the disapproval. Focusing on the criticism creates sideways energy that takes me off task and does exactly no good. So rather than argue and defend, or plead and cajole, or try to convince and persuade critics, I bless and release them. Go well with God, and may he bless you on your journey.

Sisters, this is actually possible. You are not required to engage every argument or defend your compassion. Surprise! You can just let it go and keep doing your work. No one will die. Not even you! It may feel white hot for a minute, but then the sun rises again and life goes on. Keep your eyes on the people you are serving, the issue you are discussing, the need you are addressing. There is plenty of work to do. Onward. Life is short.

Inside healthy advocacy, there is so much life! Look at all the people who care about the same thing! Look at the amazing momentum around your shared work! Thank goodness for you and all the compassionate folks working to make this world kinder, safer, more equitable, more beautiful. Don't fail to notice how many spectacular people are running this race with you, cheering you on. You can look backward at those trying to pull you in reverse, but all your best work is ahead. Eyes up, dear one. Forward is the way.

There are a million creative paths through compassion work. Some of it is embedded in policy, legislation, political activism. Other areas are served by volunteerism, raising awareness, more hands on deck. Still others catch flight with fundraising, donations, giving circles. Not to mention advocacy through proximity, time together, the touch of human kindness (women from my church spend a day a week at a housing project primarily occupied by immigrants and refugees; they just eat and play cards because these women are incredibly lonely for friends). Plain old-fashioned love is still pretty powerful.

Case in point: last year during the Austin Pride Parade, our little church took our cues from the Mama Bears, an online support group of thousands of Christian mothers of LGBTQ children, founded by Liz Dyer and expanded by Sara Cunningham, who started the Free Mom Hugs movement. It was this simple: we made posters and T-shirts and hats that looked about as professional as a middle-school pep rally, and they said things like:

FREE MOM HUGS.
FREE DAD HUGS.
FREE SISTER HUGS.
FREE GRANDMA HUGS.
FREE PASTOR HUGS.

And we stood on the side of the parade with our arms ready and waiting to hug people like it was our paying jobs. And when I say hugs, I mean the kind a mama gives her beloved kid: full frontal, tight as a vise, a beat too long but mamas will do what they want, man. Our arms were never empty. We "happy hugged" a ton of folks, but dozens of times, I'd spot someone in the parade look our way, squint at our shirts and posters, and *race* into our arms. These were the dear hearts who said:

"I miss this."
"My mom doesn't love me anymore."
"My dad hasn't spoken to me in three years."
"Please just one more hug."

You can only imagine what "Pastor Hugs" did to folks. So we told them over and over that they were impossibly loved and needed and precious. And we hugged until our arms fell off. This is what we are doing here, what we are here for. After hours in the summer sun, we all went home covered in glitter, sweat, and more than a few tears.

Like I said, plain old-fashioned love is still pretty powerful.

This harsh world can never have too many advocates pleading in favor of one another. We need you. That thing that is bursting in your chest? Listen to it. Give it energy, give it life. Circle up with the coconspirators who have the same internal thumping and go make some good trouble. Put your stake in the ground: "I care about this. I believe in the possibility of wholeness here. I am all in. I would march for this." No hiding or shirking. No prioritizing criticism or the opinions of others. Just beautiful compassion while doing work that matters for people who deserve goodness, same as anyone. You will not regret this. Build your own legacy. Have a good story to tell your great-grandchildren.

So grateful to share planet space with you, sisters.

Lace up your shoes. Your march awaits.

HOW I CONNECT

11

I WANT TO CONNECT
WITH HONESTY

A couple of years ago, I banded together with my ride-or-die friend Nichole Nordeman and our merry band of trouble-makers, and we took the Moxie Matters Tour on the road for a year and a half, well past the shelf life of most tours but nobody tells us what to do. There were nine of us, and we spent the majority of the tour on a bus together in bunks stacked three deep times four. I called it my bunk-bed coffin. It will always be one of the greatest memories of my life.

You can't travel that closely for that much time and not have some stories born out of stark, unvarnished honesty. We kept it above board for around seven-and-a-half minutes, then all bets were off. One notable moment, our guitar player Noah, one of my favorite humans, nodded at our merch manager Chrissy after hearing her tell a sports story and said sagely, "This makes sense. I knew you played softball because of your hips." When the chorus of women yelled, "*NOAH!*" he helpfully clarified by saying, "I didn't mean your hips. I meant your thighs." (This is the same Noah who asked our Indian sound engineer Stephen, "As a brown man, do your teeth also turn purple when you drink red wine?" To which Stephen replied coolly, "No. We are immune." The TOMFOOLERY.)

We got plenty of honesty on that tour, some we dished out to each other, and some we heard from attendees. Most of these disclosures were beautiful, heartfelt, the stuff of heaven. Women shared their stories and moments and secrets and victories. We still talk about them. Others shared . . . different things. Example: one of our favorite parts of the tour was the meet and greet after each show, an endless source of connection and love. Women would grab our hands and lean in to say something impossibly kind or important. Nichole and I have served women for a collective fifty years, so we have tons of history with our people. One unforgettable night, a very dear woman made it to the front of the line, put her hands on Nichole's shoulders, and, with tears wobbling in her eyes, said, "Your music helped get us pregnant."

Now, look, I'm not a songwriter and thus am unfamiliar with the various ways Christian music inspires its listeners, but apparently this disclosure even shocked Nichole because we both stood there with frozen smiles, blinking and blinking and blinking. I'm not sure when she wrote "The Unmaking" she ever guessed someone would make a baby to it. This was a lot to digest. I gave Nichole's hand a little squeeze, and she finally replied, "Well, that is a very . . . new thing to hear. I'm so pleased about . . . this interesting way I was . . . able to help." I didn't *dare* look at her, because if we locked eyes, we would lose every manner of our crap. When we got to the elevator twenty minutes later, the doors shut, we stared at each other, and then cried with laughter for ten minutes. Move over, Luther Vandross. White Christian lady worship music is the new sexy time track.

Telling someone the whole truth is a real, real thing. Sometimes shocking, sometimes jarring, I still feel proud every time I bear witness to someone laying it all out. On its face, honesty is a simple expectation of the human life: just tell the truth. It is pretty plain when we teach our kids: "Be honest" and its shadow side "Don't lie." Most of us consider ourselves people who highly value truth telling. Yet we are almost to the end of this book, and every single chapter addresses an issue or need or desire we are often not fully honest about. Some are overt, some passive aggressive, some secret, some denied, but we are actually filled with dishonesty on the regular. We love truth telling except when we don't, we practice it except when we don't, we require it except when we don't. It is okay to admit this, because it is ubiquitous to humanity.

Dr. Robert Feldman spent his career examining why people lie and found that, not only do all of us do it (and with great frequency), but we most often do it to grease the social wheels or, as he wrote in his book *The Liar in Your Life*:

> to make social interactions proceed more smoothly. People lie to be agreeable or to make us feel better about ourselves. What my research has shown is that lies occur regularly in every office. They occur regularly in every living room, in every bedroom, they occur regularly in conversations between strangers and conversations between friends. [A key] misconception is that we are relentless truth seekers. It turns out that in many cases we accept and even embrace the lies of others. In some cases, it is simply expedient to accept others' lies. And when lies are consistent with the way we wish to view ourselves as smart, competent, successful people, we're often motivated to believe the lies to which we are exposed.[1]

There is obviously a wide range of lies, from those that smooth out a social interaction all the way to calculated deception designed to mislead. Lying can also include omission, withholding on purpose, sometimes with nefarious intent and sometimes for lack of courage.

As lies are all across the spectrum, so are people. Some folks are mostly inconsequential liars with the occasional, mostly harmless niceties that lack sincerity but have no major repercussions. Others build lives chock-full of lies big and small, intentional and automatic; lying is almost a default gear and the fallout can be catastrophic. And, of course, there are numerous levels between the poles. We can likely gauge the health of our relationships based on where we fall on the scale, as chronic honesty tends to arc with trustworthiness, mature conflict resolution, and authenticity— key building blocks of healthy connections. On the other hand, chronically dishonest people generally have relationships marked by distrust, turmoil, and shallow connections. Folks primarily dishonest by omission will experience relationships tainted by their own passive aggressiveness and resentment.

Here is the problem: freedom moves out of reach when we begin to lie. You ask, "Did you get my email?" I can answer truthfully that I received it and have just not replied, or I can make myself look less thoughtless and claim I haven't. Pretty low-level evasion, but these pave the way for more consequential lies. Dr. Feldman wrote, "As soon as people feel that their self-esteem is threatened, they immediately begin to lie at higher levels."[2] We never want the gig to be up, right? With loads of us already riddled with imposter syndrome, it feels terrible to admit that we have acted lazy or irresponsible. We don't want to cop to failure or run-of-the-mill bad behavior. Nor do we like to own our anger or hurt feelings or frustration. Women are *determined* to seem agreeable, so we sacrifice honesty for conflict aversion, even when the stakes are high. Ironically, this dishonesty locks us away in solitary confinement and we are less free, not more; less connected, not more.

Often the relationships affected most dramatically are with family members. The one space we should be the safest, the most truthful, the most gracious is where many women feel disconnected. Of course, these are our most consequential relationships, the ones that absolutely matter, so areas of great health and great tension are all amplified. When my family is humming and connecting and trusting each other with big, true things, I can take on the world. When my family is disconnecting and hiding and pretending, I feel vulnerable everywhere else. There are a million reasons why a perfectly good family becomes disintegrated, but I suspect it all begins with small lies, small omissions, small pretenses.

No, I'm fine.
Yes, everything is okay at school.
No, I'm not upset.
Yes, I'm all right with this decision.
No, things are fine with my friends.
Yes, I'm happy.

"Jen," you may be saying, "my source of loneliness is my marriage. The call is coming from inside the house." Let's start here: at this very moment, Brandon and I are in marriage counseling. We have been married for twenty-five years, and here we are, needing some maintenance, *still* learning how to connect for the long haul. I understand how your most important relationship can wobble, drift, slam, or even sink. Sincerity with your partner can get bogged down by parenting and exhaustion and small slights that accrue without the antidote of consistent honesty. My instinct is to tuck all my hurt feelings away so they . . . disappear or dissolve or something

(I'm unclear on the science). But they actually calcify into a mountain of resentment which, as I'm discovering, is way harder to chip away at than a single conflict managed in the moment. Not that it is any of her business, but my counselor suggests that my lies of omission have wreaked a bit of havoc. What I pay her for is to tell me how to fix Brandon, but she insists on teaching me how to manage my daily moments with truthfulness, even though conflict with him makes me freeze on contact.

Rather than tell the truth in the moment of friction, I go backward, velcroing this latest thing to the themed board of offenses I nurture, then I go forward, trying to hustle this tension into the future where it is mercifully over. So, in other words, my internal process sounds like, "I will first cite this offense in my mental backlog, and then I will skim past this *actual* moment so I can be done with it." Brandon, on the other hand, boils wildly and immediately over, then fixes himself a snack. Healthy! I have no idea why we need the help of a therapist!

Her counsel toward me centers on mindfulness, at which I am utter rubbish. Dr. Brad Blanton calls this Radical Honesty:

> Lying is a/the primary cause of suffering: Stress, pain, oppression of self and others, even war... are primarily caused and maintained by various forms of lying (withholding, pretending, attachment to belief about what "should" be true, etc). Being honest, listening and sticking with each other is the key to improving relationships with others and improving how we feel about ourselves.
>
> Radical honesty is a pragmatic, functional path to reduce human suffering through sharing in depth and detail what you feel, what you think, what you have done, and what you want. It is a way to liberate yourself from being at the mercy of your untrustworthy reactive mind and to get to a place where you forgive other people and yourself at the same time.[3]

Essentially this is mindfulness: a nonjudgmental, zoomed-out, from-a-narrator's-perspective description of simply what IS. It includes a neutral stance toward yourself and the actual moment at hand. For me, radical honesty feels overwhelming in the moment with another person because I am typically dominated by My Feelings, so I am learning to apply these concepts internally first, then externally.

Distinguishing *noticing* from *thinking* triggers the power to connect honestly, and there is a difference. In order to stay in the moment, you need to distinguish between *what happened* and *what your mind does* with what happened. As mentioned, my mind takes to its velcro board of pinned offenses, so *simply noticing* interrupts my negative trajectory and gives each moment a chance at resolution. Radical honesty is observational using your senses: only what you see with your eyes and hear with your ears and sense in your body. It doesn't draw conclusions. It doesn't make assumptions or fill in any blanks. It notices only what is real and really happening, not the reactive meanings we typically assign based on judgments and memories. It stays in the moment and strips it of any inflated meaning, which can send a small disagreement about the toilet paper roll crashing into a five-hour standoff on fifteen years of your partner's bad habits (I've heard).

And then, you simply report out loud what you notice: what you observe, what you really think, and what you want. You still may have hard things to say observationally; mindfulness doesn't mean all offenses are only perceived. As Dr. Blanton said candidly:

> It is important to understand that the title of my book is *Radical Honesty*, not *Liberal Honesty* or *Sporadical Honesty* or *Positive Honesty* or any other horseshit like that. Eighty-five percent of relationships are pretty much more phony than authentic, half or more of marriages split up, and more than half of those that

do stay together suck. What couples need to do is be more like children in communicating and loving. Children are good at loving. [Taber Shadburne said,] The idea of this often scares the hell out of folks, because of the fear of the pain that may be involved or even a breakup. And, yes, both of these are possible, but being willing to feel your way through pain together is the cost of admission to real love and intimacy.[4]

These principles apply to other important relationships too. I have two kids in college, two in high school, and one in middle. Good reader, it has come to my attention that we got maybe two-thirds of the story when our big kids lived at home. Their stories and secrets are currently finding their way into the open air, and I feel *some kind of way about it.* Sometimes this is supposed to be funny, the kids sitting on the porch telling us when they lied and how we knew nothing. "Ha ha!" say the children. "The parents were clueless! Omg, I did that same thing! Ha ha!"

I feel around zero ha ha's about this.

But these are just the "funny" ones. We are also hearing some very dark sorrows our kids weathered unbeknownst to us. The kind of stuff that makes you want to grab all your babies and move to a deserted island where no one can ever lay eyes on them again. I can't describe how sad I am they struggled alone. I will never not be sad. I want to rewind time and rattle the cages of our family structures. I want to shake my mom radar to life. I want to redo every moment I didn't barrel right into a hard or weird or awkward conversation like a wild bull. I want to unassume all I assumed. I wish I had built a few more bunkers the kids could've found shelter in, even if they rolled their eyes during the construction. Brandon and I are taking this brave intel from our launched kids and trying to uncover blind spots with the ones still at home.

It is on parents to build a family where honesty is cherished and truth telling is protected. This cannot be implied; it certainly can't be assumed. We have to ask leading questions and weather our kids' squeamishness, because they may resist, but they actually want to be asked, parented, shielded. Carrying secrets is as detrimental to our kids' souls as it is to ours. Childhood is already lonely; hiding and disconnecting from your own parents is too dark. We can choose (read: force) solidarity with our kids during the most confusing seasons of development.

There is no magic formula for creating an honest environment outside of consistent dialogue often marked by awkwardness, even teen outrage (gird your loins, sisters). Dr. Jane Nelson suggests family meetings as one mechanism for truth telling and problem solving. There are tons of ways to structure these, but she recommends including the following (my own commentary):

THE AGENDA: This is where the family can write problems. Ask if anyone can think of any problems they'd like help with. If they can't think of anything, say, "What about _____ (whatever problem you noticed)?" Keep the agenda on the fridge and, during the week, when you notice something, you might say, "That sounds like a good one to add to the agenda." Don't insist. Just notice if they do or not.

COMPLIMENTS: During compliments, go around the circle and allow everyone to give a thank you for _____, an atta boy/girl for _____, or an appreciation for _____.

BRAINSTORMING FOR SOLUTIONS: Think of as many ideas as possible to solve the shared problems. They can be practical or wild and crazy. After the family brainstorms (with no discussion), choose one solution that everyone agrees on and try it for a week.

A FAMILY ACTIVITY OR A PLAN FOR ONE: A game, cooking,

popcorn and a movie, anything. Or make sure a cool up-coming family event gets put on the calendar.[5]

All this should take ten or fifteen minutes tops, and there is a 100 percent chance your children will balk at the whole enterprise. Of course they will! Family meetings will be "lame" and "boring"; nonetheless, you are building a family culture of truth telling and problem solving. Younger kids will learn to discuss younger problems, but that muscle memory rolls right into adolescence and adolescent problems. Perhaps one serious conundrum will be solved out of twenty, but the normalization of honesty is something your kids won't unlearn. Virtually every other message they receive is to polish it all up and post it on Instagram; you are modeling a wholehearted way of life they may not learn anywhere else.

Our friends Trina and Andrew practiced "Sunday Church" at home each weekend, and one ironclad component was this rule: "You can say absolutely anything during confession, and we will not hold it against you." Their children deeply tested their will-power by taking them at their word. Sure enough, *they confessed.* And our friends sat there and muted their faces and didn't penal-ize whatever behavior the kids divulged (where is their adult prize??). They worked through solutions and whatever natural consequences were in play, but they made disclosure safe. As a result, Trina and Andrew have healthy and transparent relation-ships with their grown kids, because not only was honesty never punished, inauthenticity was not rewarded. Our children know when we prefer their shiny, fake selves to the gritty, harder truth. They understand which version of family we like to present; the pressure we exert over their images is not a mystery. They know the score.

In our family, discussing our own failures greases the machine. Nothing opens up dialogue like saying, "When I was thirteen, me and my best friend took Grana's car around the neighborhood and ran over a mailbox." Or currently, "I really handled your pain poorly. I was scared and ashamed, and I blew it. Please forgive me. If I could do it over, I would respond like this _____." (Relationships mended by forgiveness are powerful things.) When we model honesty and apologies, our kids learn in real time how to construct a life on truth. We interrupt the toxic trajectory of *pretending* before it becomes rooted and thus a thousand times harder to pull up.

Perhaps honesty is hardest to practice in your work relationships. "In the workplace, people are continuously, and often unconsciously, assessing your communication style for two sets of qualities: warmth (empathy, likeability, caring) and authority (power, credibility, status)," wrote Carol Kinsey Goman in *Forbes.*

> There is no "best" communication style for all business interactions—and, certainly, there are many exceptions to the generalities I'm presenting—but typically women have the edge in collaborative environments where listening skills, inclusive body language and empathy are more highly valued, and men are thought to "take charge" more readily and viewed as more effective in environments where decisiveness is critical. Men are also judged to be better at monologue—women at dialogue.

In Goman's research, she found both men and women identified the same set of strengths and weaknesses in themselves and each other. For women, the top three communication strengths were

the ability to read body language and pick up nonverbal cues
good listening skills
an effective display of empathy

And the top three communication weaknesses for women were

being overly emotional
meandering (not getting to the point)
not being authoritative

As it relates to truth telling in the workplace, consider the strengths of men:

a commanding physical presence
direct and to-the-point interactions
an effective display of power

And their communication weaknesses:

being overly blunt and direct
being insensitive to audience reactions
being too confident in their own opinion[6]

In another published study, professors Vinita Mohindra and Samina Azhar call this "rapport behavior" (women) versus "report behavior" (men).[7] This is painting with a wide brush, obviously, but the fault lines suggest that women speak honestly at work far less than men. Clearly not all bad, as our strengths value diplomacy, which has its place, but women are perceived as indirect and less confident. While deeply skilled at reading a room, we undervalue truth telling, which, notice, is something *both* genders respect in men (I cannot quit thinking about this). We've convinced ourselves honesty at work will be poorly received, yet the data suggests people prefer direct communication.

Our instincts steer us away from high levels of honesty at work, and while wisdom includes discretion, perhaps we've placed too high a premium on conflict avoidance. While it may feel unwise to reply to your boss who has just asked for (fill in the blank) that you think the task is demeaning or a poor use of time, Dr. Blanton argues that is precisely when radical honesty allows you to talk about perceived condescension in the relationship or how you might better manage your time or why you aren't invested enough in your work. Some of the suspected fallout from workplace truth telling is invented. A good boss or team leader or coworker wants to know where his or her staff is unhappy or wasting company time.

We've created binary options that aren't real. It is quite possible to prioritize direct communication at work without being an ass. Frankly, women are best set up for this balance, because we are empathetic communicators and better at interpreting nonverbal cues. We are already good with people; we just need to apply our relational skills to challenging workplace conversations. I suspect it is tougher for men to reverse-engineer their weaknesses, as tempering with sensitivity or humility is harder than just adding candor.

Brandon and I have learned tons from each other in this space. He manages the lion's share of my business development, including communication with my team members and staff. We implemented this role change last year, because my leadership style was simply too indirect (yes, I am writing a chapter out of my own deficiencies, because *I'm still learning things, too, you guys*). Several areas in my career were either stagnant or unproductive, and I failed to make the necessary changes even though some were super obvious. If I had a dime for every time Brandon said to me, "Jen, THIS IS BUSINESS, not a BFF Convention." Here is the funny thing: my partners actually prefer his direct, clear communication to whatever fluffy nonsense I was keeping the ship afloat with. In mere months, he put gas in the engine of several stalled ventures, and they sparked to life, every one of them. He made needed staff changes, moved a bunch of pieces around, trimmed some fat, and increased overall team morale. My too-passive approach actually hurt the team rather than helped.

While I'm learning to employ greater honesty with my partners, I have also been able to coach Brandon, as no one ever wasted the adjective "sensitive" on him. (I do this same thing with my agent, Curtis, cut from the same just-get-to-it cloth with no love lost for girly niceties. He is a lawyer in a black-and-white world. He spent a whole weekend teaching his son how to itemize bills for tax codes. Party guy!) Because it is vital to me that my partners feel respected and appreciated, because *they deeply are*, I've walked my guys through a few communication tools that protect warmth without sacrificing assertiveness. We learn from each other, and I daresay we've migrated to a healthier balanced middle where the Team Mom has become more direct and the Team Mobsters have become more sensitive.

You know immediately if you are withholding honesty in your career; it will be the thing that sits in your gut like a rock. Maybe it includes being overlooked or undervalued. It is no secret that women are disadvantaged professionally. Compared to full-time white men (the highest earners) in similar fields, full-time white women make eighty cents on the dollar, black women sixty-two, and Hispanic women fifty-seven.[8] If the wage gap improves at the same rate it has the last fifty years, white women will achieve pay parity in 2059, black women in 2119, and Hispanic women will have to wait until 2224.[9] So yeah. You're not making it up.

Perhaps your workplace drama has more to do with complicated relationships or task-related tension. All normal! Our places of work are full of people, and things go sideways all the time. This doesn't make your job beyond repair or necessitate a career change. If you are unhappy, may I gently ask if you have done all you can do to effect meaningful change? Have you broached a hard conversation? Have you been honest with your boss or coworker? Have you discussed your concerns with relevant people? What if you gave your colleagues the benefit of the doubt and assumed they are also interested in satisfied employees, thriving bottom lines, healthy team morale, and innovation? What if the worst-case scenario you've been avoiding turns out to be an honest conversation that effects the exact change you want?

Even if it doesn't, wouldn't you rather be honest in your work life and have some agency over your own career experience? Is your silence worth the turmoil? With good communication skills applied, resolution may be easier than you think or, in any case, possible. Remember, the research says both men and women appreciate direct communication and find it admirable, not confrontational.

A greater degree of honesty in our key relationships, families, and workplaces would have monumental effects. Alice Walker said, "The most common way people give up their power is by thinking they don't have any."[10] We actually hold enormous power over our connections. Until we have pulled the lever of compassionate truth telling, we don't even know how our relationships could transform. This is just a better way to live, sisters.

Most primary alliances can survive even the most brutal honesty; silent complacency is the kiss of death. When there is no fight left, no urgency to tell the truth or hear it, not enough self-respect to act with agency nor enough respect for others to respond to theirs, that is the real problem. More relationships drift into indifference than capsize from conflict. Practicing honesty and not overfearing confrontation is the mark of healthy people and their subsequently successful partnerships. The honest folks also learn how to forgive and ask forgiveness, so it has a boomerang effect on our relational health; it all rises together.

Truth is the epicenter of everything good. From it flows courage, kindness, maturity, humility, happiness. It leaves nothing on the table and thus purges our lives of regret or, just as bad, resentment.

It dethrones toxic trends from reigning in our relationships: pretending, faking, lying—the most terrible enemies of flourishing lives.

Trust truth. Trust it to do what it has always done. Trust it to work over the lesser but easier tactic of acting. Trust its proven results to move your relationships closer to vibrancy, not further. Just telling the truth is healing. It is an end unto itself. It feels good to say what you mean, taking better, kinder care of the person across from you in doing so. Now they are dealing with a real person. Now you both can get somewhere. People of faith, truth is our cornerstone for a reason; God can do immeasurable work with your honesty. After all, this is the same God who said, "Come on now, let's discuss this together . . ."

Give truth a fighting chance to work its magic. Do it for the people you love. Do it for the work you love.

Do it for yourself.

12

I WANT TO CONNECT
WITHOUT DRAMA

This is a picture of my grandpa, who went to Jesus a few years ago. This picture communicates a few things he and all the other members of the Greatest Generation are not here for:

Shenanigans
Wasting time
Wasting words
Selfies
The internet
Cell phones
Netflix

Instagram filters
Man buns
Artisan soap
The Kardashians
US *Weekly*
Seatbelts
$6 coffee
Cauliflower rice
Backtalk
Dog outfits
Buzzfeed
Coachella
Self-care
Clapping in church
Paying too much attention to children
Art history degrees
Advil
Being a damn fool

My grandpa would be here for none of it. If any of us are tempted to fill our hours with nonsense, I suggest we print this picture off and hang it by our laptops. Please peep at his hard-core leather vest, which suggests that we take our horsecrap ELSEWHERE.

Look, this man wore a gentleman's fedora in his nursing home nearly every day while other people's great-grandmas threw themselves at him. The nursing home director called my mom once to let her know that Grandpa woke up with a lady caller in his bed, but the saucy senior in question told my mom later not to worry, because "she was a Christian lady." You better believe none of that was going on Instagram, because my grandpa had game and it was not for public consumption, you animals. So savage.

While I am very much here for Instagram filters and Advil, I share my grandpa's contempt for drama. No thank you, Universe. I've tasted the fruit of hogwash, and it's going to be a hard pass from me. I like this topic for the last chapter, because it is a summation of everything else: Dear World, I'm here with my girls, and we've all decided against your unnecessary foolishment. You can miss us with that flimflam.

Let's define drama, because, as you know, I am loathe to derail into straw-man arguments. What I mean by drama are relationships or scenarios that are consistently one-sided, manipulative, disingenuous, self-sunk, irresponsible, untrustworthy, unsafe, overly critical, or flat-out mean. A peer who constantly wants you to parent her. A "friend" who treats you like garbage. A group that endlessly gossips. A church that peddles shame. A colleague who takes credit for your work. A roommate who is never sorry and always right. A family member who refuses healthy boundaries. A neighbor who repeatedly betrays your confidence. A kid driving the Crazy Train straight through your house every day. A spouse acting more like your child . . . or your parent. An environment or platform or social media outlet that reads like a *Real Housewives* quagmire.

Before the yeah-buts, consider this from Drs. Cloud and Townsend in *Safe People*:

> No one is perfect. Safe people will at times stumble and be "unsafe" for, after all, they are sinners too. So do not expect perfection. Instead, when you are measuring someone's character, look at these traits in terms of degree. Everyone lies at some time or in some way. But not everyone is a pathological liar. Look for degrees of imperfection . . . There are many good people out there. To find them, make sure you use discernment, wisdom, and information, and trust your experience with people. If someone is destructive or producing bad fruit in your

life, be careful. Keep looking, praying, and seeking until you find safe people—people who will give you all the benefits that God has planned for you.[1]

There is a big difference between a normal mess-up between otherwise healthy folks and a relationship defined by drama. There is a big difference between someone in a season of great need and one in a bottomless pit of need, particularly of their own making. "I hurt you and I blew it" is not the same as "You know I didn't mean that. You're always so sensitive." If she is constantly gossiping *to* you, she is constantly gossiping *about* you. Not all groups of adult women act like middle schoolers. And people in healthy relationships are not always frustrated, disappointed, exhausted, or resentful—clues that something is definitely amiss. Like Victor Frankl wrote in *Man's Search for Meaning*, "An abnormal reaction to an abnormal situation is normal behavior."[2] Drama makes us bananas. You're not crazy.

I am forty-five and, at this point, my life is remarkably drama-free. Obviously, this doesn't include randoms who create giant messes online, or drama that just happens because That's Life, but as for the people I've invited deeply into my world, I am surrounded by healthy folks. This curating process took years. Without an ounce of Mean Girl Tricks (I don't subscribe to those ever), I've purged some toxic friends and groups (or behaviors—more on that in a minute) from the inner circle, and my only regret is I didn't do it sooner. This is not fancy, but I applied these questions to my relationships or environments and noticed a clear separation:

Is this relationship mainly one-sided? I had a few friendships where I was always the listener, always the giver, always the problem solver. I would answer one question to every one hundred I would ask. It didn't actually feel like a friendship, more like a transaction. I always left feeling depleted and not seen.

Does this person lie or gossip too much? Look, everyone does a little of this, but I'm not about to be lied to on the regular and call that normal. And unrelenting gossips terrify me. Some women are simply untrustworthy, and life is too short for that nonsense. I will deliver exactly zero fodder for your notorious rumor mill.

Does this person create constant drama, then expect everyone else to fix it? A friend of mine literally ran through two dozen of us until there was no one left. After the ten-thousandth self-imposed crisis, I realized I was not a friend but an enabler. As Cloud and Townsend say, "You are responsible *to* others, not *for* others." We get what we tolerate.

In general, am I becoming kinder, wiser, stronger, and more joyful around this person or group? Or meaner, critical, fragile, and unhappy? Do I like myself more or less in this space? Does she call forth my best or bring out my worst? While my behavior is on me, our closest influences matter. (This filter is why I spend the least amount of time on Twitter, where kindness goes to die.)

I have at some point failed every one of these tests, and so have my closest people—but as exceptions, not the rule. Even if I didn't carefully log relational history, my gut would give me the same conclusions. So does yours. You know the relationships that give you life and those that drain it. This is not a real riddle.

At some point, if you are serious about opting out of unnecessary drama, you decide to say out loud, "I'm not doing this anymore." You erect healthy boundaries which, in some cases, can salvage a relationship from the rubble of codependency. It means dropping *your own behaviors* that allowed a connection to splinter: fear of confrontation, fear of loss, doing too much, rescuing, saying yes when you mean no, putting up with terrible treatment, pride, control.

I'd love to insert the entire contents of *Boundaries* here, the best book I've ever read on this subject, but to avoid that tricky plagiarism, I want to touch on two of the "Ten Laws of Boundaries" that Cloud and Townsend outlined to help us discern the principles of boundaries and how to apply them.

First, the Law of Sowing and Reaping:

> Sometimes people don't reap what they sow, because someone else steps in and reaps the consequences for them. Rescuing a person from the natural consequences of his behavior enables him to continue in irresponsible behavior. The Law of Sowing and Reaping has not been repealed. It is still operating. But the doer is not suffering the consequences; someone else is. Today we call a person who continually rescues another person a codependent. In effect, codependent, boundaryless people "cosign the note" of life for the irresponsible people in their lives . . . Note: *confronting* an irresponsible person is not painful to him; only consequences are.[3]

It is not selfish to allow an irresponsible person to lay in the bed he or she made. Women, especially Christian women, have a terrible fear of being self-centered. We've been told to put others first our entire lives. This is a general biblical principle that creates a flourishing earth, but the very same Bible is full of people reaping what they sowed. It is not a carte blanche order to always pay someone else's overdrawn bill. We actually rob people of growth when we shoulder the brunt of their consequences. My children learned their most concrete lessons by being grounded, paying for the damage they caused, forfeiting the phone they abused, rebuilding the fence they destroyed, going without when they spent all their money. Them's the breaks, kids. This is how responsibility works. If someone gets to pass the buck with no repercussions, this has a devastating cumulative effect not only on relationships but on his or her own maturity.

Second, the Law of Exposure:

Your boundaries need to be made visible to others and communicated to them in relationship. We have many boundary problems because of relational fears. We are beset by fears of guilt, not being liked, loss of love, loss of connection, loss of approval, receiving anger, being known, and so on . . . Because of these fears, we try to have secret boundaries. We withdraw passively and quietly instead of communicating an honest no to someone we love. We secretly resent instead of telling someone that we are angry about how they have hurt us. Often we will privately endure the pain of someone's irresponsibility instead of telling them how their behavior affects us and other loved ones, information that would be helpful to their soul . . . If our boundaries are not communicated and exposed directly, they will be communicated indirectly or through manipulation . . . When our boundaries are in the light, that is, are communicated openly, our personalities begin to integrate for the first time.[4]

The most crucial thing about boundaries is this: they are about you, not the other person. They are not about controlling or changing his behavior, although they may have that effect. They are not about punishing someone. They are not mean or selfish or retaliatory. Boundaries might not change anyone else's behavior at all. The only thing they guarantee is what you will or will not do, what you will or will no longer put up with, what you will or will not accommodate. That's it. Boundaries are entirely about you. They are calm, clear words backed up with calm, clear actions:

If you yell at me, I will leave the room/house. I will talk to you when you are calm.

*I can no longer watch your kids every time you mismanage your
    schedule.*

No, I won't pay your bills again.

*If you come home drunk, the kids and I will stay at my mom's
    that night and tell her why.*

*You hired me for twenty hours a week and gave me forty hours of
    work. Which twenty would you like done?*

This simply transfers the reaping to the sower. That's all. This
is how the world works. It is how we learn and mature and become
real adults. You are not paying the tab for someone else's drama,
irresponsibility, manipulation, or offenses. The chips fall where
they should—chips are powerful incentives for growth!—and you
will no longer enable the behavior.

Expect this to go terribly. Nobody likes to be on the receiving end of healthy boundaries, because when someone else cleans
up our mess, we get to maintain the fake version of ourselves as
nonproblematic. We are allowed to keep acting poorly without consequences. We don't suffer the ill effects of our own poor planning,
addictions, unfair expectations, overspending, bullying, tantrums,
or bad choices; why would we ever change the system? It is working
for us! (When Brandon and I downloaded a program that turned
our kids' data off after consistent disregard of house rules, it was
like Armageddon. *We were utter dictators.*)

When you first put calm, clear boundaries on the behavior
of someone else, he or she will most likely hate it. He might call
you selfish, coldhearted, greedy. She may accuse you of hatred,
abandonment, ungodliness. You might be blamed for his financial collapse, career crash, ruined reputation. People are loathe to
admit their own failures, so blaming their enablers for pulling out
of the game is an easy reach. With boundaries in place, it will likely
get worse before it gets better, if it gets better at all. But even if it

doesn't, you are not in charge of outcomes. Neither are you in control of someone else's choices. Only yours.

In the highly unlikely case that one of my readers *is* the difficult person, here is good news: it is never too late to become safer, more considerate, more responsible. There are a million reasons why adults disrespect boundaries and take advantage of the people around us. It is easy to draw straight lines from our childhood experiences to the way we function as adults. And, as I mentioned, all of us create drama sometimes.

But truth is *your* friend here too. You have the same power to directly communicate with someone you have wronged. You can be the brave person in the equation and say, "I have . . .

> taken advantage of you . . .
> taken you for granted . . .
> expected too much . . .
> blamed you for my poor choices . . .
> not been a good friend . . .
> been unsafe . . .
> been unkind . . .

. . . and I want to ask forgiveness. Would you be willing to talk frankly about how I have made you feel?" Remember, humans are not naturally good at honesty. You may need to give someone permission several times before he or she is willing to tell you the truth, especially if your relationship has been marked by enabling behavior. If you have been difficult to confront, this conversation may seem unsafe to the other person. Cloud and Townsend suggest two questions to regularly ask the closest people in your life:

What do I do that draws you toward me?

What do I do that pushes you away?

Dear ones, I have asked these questions and will readily admit the answers can be hard to hear. However,

> the truth increases love. People who are free to be honest are free to love each other. This is because the fear of loss of attachment is gone. You'll hear insights, perceptions, emotions, and observations you may have never expected. When people feel truly free to tell the truth, they tend to be quite honest but also quite loving. Remember, your safe person has heard you take the initiative to ask for the truth. There exists no concrete wall of denial to break through. The more rigorous you are with your own self-examination, the better it goes for you. And the converse is true: the more you minimize your failings, the more your safe people have to work in sharing the truth with you. Get real, get honest, and get working on yourself.[5]

You are not stuck. You, too, can opt out of drama, even when you have created it. Listen to me: your path out is truth. When we shatter all the lies that duct-tape relationships together, tell the full truth, and hear the full truth, healing is possible, even in the most broken connections. It is POWERFUL to admit wrongdoing, ask forgiveness, offer forgiveness, discuss healthy boundaries and learn to respect them, take ownership of your own choices. Powerful! If you have never applied these tools, your relationships have not even sniffed their potential. You are just as capable as anyone to embrace truth and get free.

Drama is not a life sentence. Boundaries are potent corrective tools to help transform relationships into their healthiest version. They are also sometimes sifting tools that identify toxic relationships or environments to walk away from. This is your work, sister, your responsibility. Maybe you need to set them. Maybe you need to respect someone else's. One way or another, you are reaping what you are sowing. If your relationships are laden with hogwash, it is time to look in the mirror.

My friend Faitth lived in Austin for several years before moving to North Carolina. As one of the few black women in our church at the time, we had many conversations about White Church and Black Church, both of which Faitth had been embedded in at one time or another. Once, while discussing *yet another* of our sermon series on mission/this broken world/serving accompanied by *yet another* Somber White Guy with a Guitar worship set (#whitechurchsowhite), she said, "Y'all. I love you. I do. But sometimes I just need some victory!" (This is now our baseline as a church board: *Guys, where is the victory in this series? I detect zero victory.*)

Dear reader, our lives need some victory! To a huge degree, we can opt out of drama and into connected, meaningful relationships that light us up. Into safer, more equitable relationships mended by fair boundaries. This is all incredibly possible. Life is so freaking short. I can't believe how fast it is going. With all my being, I don't want to get to the end of it clutching a shred of anger or resentment. I don't want to die having left things unsaid. I want to feel saturated and rich and grateful. I hope to look back on all my years and see a husband and children and grandchildren and friends and neighbors and a faith community and world that I wildly loved. I want a legacy dripping with human connection, up to its eyeballs in memories and adventures and weathered storms and gladness. I hope to leave a wake of victory, a life of full integrity. I want to say it all, risk it all, own it all.

We don't have to be scared. Truth is the front door to the life we've always wanted to build. It creates safety for the people we love most on this planet. It bursts through the door and says, "HELLO, WORLD! HERE I AM!" Truth allows us to be exactly who we are, how we are, walking around in these beautiful bodies with these beautiful minds. It never asks us to be anything except real as real can be; it doesn't lie or ask us to.

Truth is on the side of good and right things. It doesn't imprison us alone when life gets hard but rather hands us the keys and walks us back outside to the sunshine. Truth is a faithful defender against the lies meant to break us; it is ever on our side. Truth helps us set a gorgeous table for the deepest connections, the most absurd displays of love. It never asks us to pretend when we are lonely. It is our chief guide to joy.

Truth is exactly how we bring forth our exquisite gifts to serve this world to make it brighter in every way. It is the source material for the dreams every last one of us carry; it's all in there, worthy. It is super pumped about what we love and what we are good at. It isn't at odds with ambition. Truth selects the best threads to weave our lives together and decides which ones belong to someone else. Sometimes in our best interests, it says no.

Truth holds this line from generation to generation: Jesus is love, in him is life, through him is great joy, everyone belongs. It isn't afraid of our questions; it is not insecure or fragile. Press hard on truth. It will hold. It sends us to the front lines, because, until everyone belongs, we've replaced truth with a lie, because truth values every human equally; it favors no hierarchies. Like a miracle, truth continues to set people free; this is one of its greatest strengths. Jesus is true, and the world he envisioned is the whole truth.

Truth heals our marriages, raises up mighty children, fortifies our friendships. It is the primary connective tissue between human people; we can't function without it. Truth is sometimes hard to hear, and yet it grows us up if we'll listen. It is sometimes hard to say, and yet it grows up our relationships if we'll say it. We can build healthy families and communities and churches on truth. It is a harbor. It can handle the human part of our humanity.

Telling the truth, receiving the truth, prioritizing the truth, living the truth—this is our victory! There is no other way to live free. This is it. This is our path. C. S. Lewis said, "You can't go back and change the beginning, but you can start where you are and change the ending."[6] We absolutely can become more genuine women, proud of who we are, thrilled about where we are going, grateful for the skin we live in. We can say hard things and quit lying. We can tell the truth and experience all the freedom that comes with it. Being scared is just not a good enough reason to keep pretending. Do you notice that fear doesn't deliver? Truth is worth its salt, and it feels good to work with its power, not against it. Trust its grain; it knows what it's doing.

Grateful to be your sister. Beyond proud to run our leg of the race with you. I feel impossibly hopeful about the world we are demanding for our sons and daughters; they'll get to stand on the victories we fought for, just like we stood on those provided for us. What's true will last. History usually tells it right. A culture is only as healthy as its most wholehearted members, and it is a privilege to be true-faced with you in our time. I love who you are, and I thank you for offering nothing less than your whole, sincere, remarkable self. What a lucky world.

FINAL THOUGHTS

As discussed, I have five children, which is an entire starting basketball team. The oldest can buy beer, the youngest is wrapping up eighth grade, and I would like to nominate myself for numerous awards for surviving middle school six times, including my own traumatic experience with Mrs. Anderson and one catastrophic disaster when I left my diary in the house we moved out of and the new kid who moved in found it, read it, and brought it to school where everyone read seventeen emotional, descriptive pages about my first kiss with Gary Whipple while playing Three Minutes in the Closet. "You'll miss this" is a damn lie. Middle school is the worst time to be alive in the span of a human life, God bless and keep those weirdos.

Anyway, I am experiencing a tapered-off phenomenon called #fifthkid. I mercilessly, furiously shamed my parents for their #fourthkid approach to parenting my brother, but now I understand my mom's defense: "The thing that happened is that we got tired." I figured we were in trouble when we accidentally missed Sydney's Senior Awards Banquet, where she apparently received several, including a scholarship, because we were all at the movies watching *Avengers*. And she was just our #secondkid. I knew at that point we would probably look at Remy one day and say, "So, are you a senior? Or a junior or no? Are you still enrolled? Did we apply for any colleges? Do you still live upstairs?"

In big families, older kids are like middle management to help raise the younger ones. First kids get parented. Last kids get fed. I figure, the oldest got 100 percent of us, middles around 50, and the youngest are in God's hands. Once middle management moves out, they call home and say things like, "Mom, are you making sure Remy wraps her hair at night? Did you teach her how to use tampons? Are you making sure she doesn't eat too much candy?" Oh my gosh, bossy! Yes! Or, like, probably.

There is an upside for the babies, because the #fifthkid gets a lot more yeses, more twenty-dollar bills, more cake for dinner, which the bigs got never. All the stuff we obsessed over with the older kids turned out to belong in a category called "None of This Really Matters," so we now operate at about half capacity on rules and such. By the #fifthkid, our parenting mantra is: *It kind of all works out. Everyone just live their lives.*

Our bigs were home on break recently and overheard me tell Remy, "Sure, Ella can spend the night," but as it was, um, a school night, they a tiny bit lost their minds.

"What? Are you kidding me? I never had a sleepover on a school night in my life! What is this?"

"Are you guys, like, not even trying anymore?"

Before I could defend myself, Remy answered calmly:

"This is who Mom is now."

THANK YOU, QUEEN. You are my favorite #fifthkid.

Reader, I'm thinking about you and *who you are now too.* Thank you for hanging in this far; self-discovery and disclosure involves hard work, and I'm grateful to have walked some of it with you. I suspect my original hypothesis was right, that some of these chapters hit you squarely between the eyes and others didn't apply at all. I bet you found really healthy parts of your life and a few spots that rub, maybe one or two that needed to be entirely rebuilt. I have a vision that if we keep at this work, this book would become obsolete. Or, if you read it again one year from now, two years from now, you'd need way less of it. I hope one day you read a note you wrote in the margin somewhere and can barely remember how lonely you felt then, how silenced, how worried. I look forward to charting my own process, too, as I felt deeply lacking in two areas and below average in another as I wrote this.

Henri Nouwen said, "I do not yet know what I carry in my heart, but I trust it will emerge as I write."[1] For me, the practice of putting pen to paper creates an alchemy hard to duplicate any other way. Something about writing it down helps bring it to life. Committing to something with written words makes it more real, more memorable. And so, let's leave this book with our own HELLO, WORLD! manifesto, a series of twelve statements from the five categories we've been discussing: this is who I am, this is what I need, this is what I want, this is what I believe, and this is how I connect. Where there was confusion, I hoped to lead toward clarity. Where there was fear, I hoped to lead toward courage.

You have twelve statements. Some of them may be common knowledge, some private, some secret, some brand new. Integration means your inside voice, your outside actions, your thoughts and beliefs, your dreams and hopes—all being in alliance. You are telling the truth. This is who you are at all times with all people. You aren't pretending or hiding. You decide to be your whole real self, and I can tell you right now, you will not regret this. This is freedom.

To help you get started identifying yours, I'll offer up mine. My twelve statements look like this:

- I am wired as a motivated, high-functioning introverted Enneagram Three. I love leading but have to work harder on self-assessment and emotions. I have a strong prophetic nature. When I'm healthy, I'm authentic and care deeply for people. When I'm disintegrating, I overvalue success and clamor for approval.

- I take up a large amount of space, because I am jammed with ideas, convictions, and dreams. I like big experiences. I like big feelings and big spaces. I'm comfortable with a large capacity and plan to fill it.

- I want to honor my body as the loyal, strong companion she is. I have been hateful to her for most of my life, and I am determined to love her better.

- I deserve goodness, even in religious spaces where I am an outlier. I am still a good sister and God's kid, and I don't deserve mischaracterization, rejection, and gossip.

- I have learned to ask for help, and thus my life is as well-manned with partners and managers as it ever has been. I feel very supported.

- I am incredibly connected to my friends and family. This is one of the greatest areas of health in my life.

- My dream is to lead millions of women toward lives of great meaning. I care about their souls, their families, their gifts, their churches, and their communities. I also have a side dream of working with food (cookbooks, travel writing, cooking show, I don't know! It's a side dream, guys!).

- I have been careless with a few yeses, which created awkward interactions and messy clean-ups for my assistant and team. This is lazy, thoughtless behavior that needs to change. I have two clear nos to give right now that I've held in purgatory with maybes.

- One biblical concept I am curious about right now is the many interpretations of heaven and hell. I'm being challenged by the diverse scholarship around an idea I've only understood one possible way.

- I would march for the eradication of white supremacy, LGBTQ rights and dignity, gun reform, women's safety and equality worldwide, a safe family for every child, and the end of human trafficking.
- I am too indirect a communicator with my husband. I want to be honest and present in every moment instead of stuck in the past or rushing to the future. I also need to be more direct with my staff and team. I've not been as good a leader as they need.
- The one place I can still occasionally get sucked into drama is online, and although I've grown here, I always regret biting back or being snarky or joining a pile-on. While not bailing on important discussions and even disagreements, I am opting out of online drama when it is mean and unproductive.

There it is. That is pretty much all the things. If you follow me online, you basically know all this already, which makes me proud. A good indicator of integration is a lack of secrets. While there is a key difference between secrecy, which is marked by shame, and privacy, which is marked by discretion, when the majority of my life is transparent, I feel at my most healthy. I feel the least scared. I experience the assimilation truth telling creates, and it is too liberating to go back.

I want you to write down your twelve statements at whatever varying degrees of integration they are in. So grab a journal and make this real! You may write something for the first time. Or identify specific relationships, decisions, or beliefs that need the warm light of honesty. Perhaps you write them today and begin speaking them soon; don't tarry too long—time cools resolution. Start small: one area, one truth, tell one safe person. Develop muscle memory for authenticity. Learn its rhythms. Practice standing firmly in it. See how it feels liberated from the confines of your mind and out in the wild. I'll warn you: becoming integrated is contagious. You'll lose your capacity for pretending. What might feel radical at first will eventually become a required way to live. Don't be afraid; this is good for literally everyone you love in your life. They deserve the true version of you. We all do.

Your truest self in its fullness—quirks, talents, dreams, beliefs, all—is an irreplaceable gift to this world. It is so beautifully and wildly gorgeous. There is not one good reason to hide any of it. Bring it forth. Let us know the real, whole you. Own it, embrace it, declare it all. Step up and out in truth; we are waiting. We need you. Every molecule of who you are, every experience you have ever had, every dream you were made to chase, every place you were designed to serve—we are all out here waiting for you with open arms. Without question:

You are fierce.
You are free.
You are full of fire.

I am cheering you on in every way, dear sister.

ACKNOWLEDGMENTS

There is a good freaking reason authors include acknowledgments, and that is because we are hopeless humans without the company of people who surround us and keep the wheels on. Let's get serious: we type for a living. It takes a village to support us with our obvious lack of useful skills. We would have all died on the Oregon Trail.

This book, particularly, is not just thanks to my current community but also forty-five years of mentorship and investment. Many people in my little world have been playing a long game with me, and thank God for their endurance.

First thanks goes to my readers. Some of you are brand-new to this circus, and some of you have stuck with me for *fifteen years*. Listen, I sincerely, really love you. I am protective of you, proud of you, and inspired by you. If you are still with me, all the way to FFaFoF, then we are basically married at this point. I will serve you with gladness until death do us part.

I have four subcommunities that mean the world to me. With so much gratitude to my Launch Team, the Jen Hatmaker Book Club, my EFs (Email Friends), and my *For the Love Podcast* listeners. We have the grandest connections in our little weirdo corners of the Hatmaker world. Between our inside jokes, billions of conversations, shared books, and in-real-life meetups, you have filled my cup to overflowing more than I can ever describe. You are so loved by this girl.

Next up: my loyal, dogged, overly generous team at Thomas Nelson. *Fierce* is our third book together, and I could not begin to calculate how many hours you have spent on Jen Hatmaker. Listen here: you stuck by me when I needed someone to stick desperately, and I will never, never forget it. For your endless work and enthusiasm, for your constant labor to bring my dreams to life, from the bottom of my heart I thank: Mark Schoenwald, Don Jacobson, Jamie Lockard, Tim Paulson, Karen Jackson, Rachel Tockstein, Janene MacIvor, Belinda Bass, and my editor Jessica Wong (thank you for letting me keep 59 percent of my swears). What a formidable squad. I adore you. In honor of Brian Hampton, our beloved friend and leader: I miss you every day, Brian. Rest well, faithful servant.

My two literary agents, Curtis Yates and Mike Salisbury, deserve every kudo in the universe. I am Whitney Houston, and you are my bodyguards (I'm not sure who my stalker is. At this point the metaphor breaks down). You have steadily helped me plow through new fields with incredible chutzpah. Whatever heart attacks I've inflicted, you never let on. I trust you, I thank you, and I love you. Everything about my career changed in your hands. You are good men, good husbands and dads, and remedial GIF users but I appreciate your efforts.

To my assistant and partner in every way, Amanda Duckett: I recently told Brandon, "If I had to choose between you and Amanda . . . well, you and I had a good run. Godspeed, sir." At this point, I don't know how I ever lived without you. If I started listing everything you do, know, handle, manage, intersect, troubleshoot, develop, execute, plan, and predict, I'd have to add one hundred pages to the end of this book. Since I'm doing movie metaphors apparently, this is *The Firm* and you can never leave. Is this a death threat? An aggressive flex admittedly, but I just love you. Thank you for everything under the sun and moon.

Sending so much gratitude to my cocreator of the *For the Love Podcast*, producer Laura Neutzling and her outstanding team of magic makers: Christine Nishiguchi, Amy Kerr, and Rodney Brown. When we sat across from each other at Brooklyn's on Main Street and carefully tested the waters with each other over chicken salads, who knew we'd be 20 million downloads down the road together soon? You are the brains, the muscles, and the backbone of our podcast, and I have never loved creating something so much. You'll always be my favorite Voice Over Lady no matter what the internet said. #volforever

To Amy Chandy and her team of kickass boss ladies: Chrissy Shelton, Anna Trent, Rachel Watkins, Amanda Garcia, Jami Belew, plus a few kickass boss fellas, Pepper Sweeney, Ray Garcia, and Stephen Mathew. You brought to life virtually everything I dreamed up for five years: six straight tours, the Jen Hatmaker Book Club, the *For the Love Podcast*, and ten thousand business initiatives. There is no one, and I mean NO ONE I'd get on a tour bus with time and again other than you people. Whenever I want to sing '80s karaoke at 2:00 a.m. at Bar Marley in deserted Knoxville, you're my first dial. I love you so much. Thank you for your endless work, unflinching enthusiasm, and your embarrassing belief in me.

A very enormous thanks goes to Dr. Jessica Frye, my friend and colaborer who painstakingly combed through, condensed, and compiled thousands of pages of research for this book. You were the most overqualified "research assistant" in the history of literature, and you brought your considerable skills as a therapist to bear on every page. As you sent the final file, you included a small note: "My cancer is back." And then you proceeded to counsel our family through a year of loss and pain. I have never known a more remarkable woman. With a deep bow, I dedicate the title of this book to you, its perfect embodiment. I love you dearly.

When I think of fierce, free, and fiery women, my mind also turns to five of the best friends in my whole life, my ASSS sisters (this is a weird thing, don't worry about it): Sarah Bessey, Sarah Goodfellow, Kristen Howerton, Tara Livesay, and Jamie Wright. The five of you hold some information unknown to any other living human. If Voxer ever releases its contents to the public, we are all going to jail. We have celebrated to the ends of the galaxy and grieved in the lowest pits of hell's sorrows together. I now know we can and will handle anything. In loving memory of Jamison, I celebrate his mama and her sisters. God, I love you.

Basically every chapter of this book has been incubated in real life with a gaggle of girlfriends I don't deserve, mentioned all throughout. Some of these friends go back twenty-seven years, some as recently as two, but every one of them knows where the bodies are buried: Jenny, Shonna, Trina, Leslie, Megan, Steph, Amy, Laura, Christi, Jessica, Karen, Jill, Jen, and my wild sisters, Lindsay and Cortney. We've done the work inside this book together in real time. Your print is on every page, every lesson, every inch of forward progress. When I try to envision my life without you in it, my mind goes blank, like that one time I accidentally told Trace about his/ our surprise trip to Tulum then just sat there blinking like a pigeon until Jenny swooped in with a masterful lie to cover it up. I love you weirdos with all my guts. Thanks for a closet full of sweatshirts.

And now bringing it all the way home: when I was two years old, an older church lady gave my mom a copy of *The Strong-Willed Child* so let's not act shocked that I wrote a book called *Fierce, Free, and Full of Fire* forty-three years later. It occurs to me that, had my parents followed today's rules for wrangling children into submission, I may have become fragile, flattened, and full of fear instead.

Since the day I was born, you let me be me in all my determined, emotional, headstrong ways, Mom and Dad. You never muzzled me. You never one time gave me the impression that I was too much. I was absolutely free to flourish because you loved your strong-willed child so well. If I had to choose two parents out of the entire scope of history, I'd pick you.

Then to the family I made. Ben at the dinner table last night: "Someone told me you write some stories about us in your books." I replied, "Some?? I write TONS of stories about you! Work it out with your therapists!" To Gavin, Sydney, Caleb, Ben, and Remy, you are the reason I am happy, fulfilled, and gray-haired (underneath my expensive hair dye). I am so proud of you, exactly how you are. I wouldn't change one thing. You're growing up and launching as fierce, free young adults full of fire, and my heart could just burst.

Brandon, look at this crew of ours. Remember that time you found me in an empty bathtub fully clothed staring at the wall because I was sure we weren't getting out of middle school alive? We got out. Thank you for a quarter of a century of The Good Life together. Thank you for believing in me way before it made sense. Thank you for blessing my work and my voice and my path with no equivocation. Thank you for loving me twenty-six years after we first made out in your red Pontiac LeMans at the Shawnee Park.

Finally, I want to thank Jesus. (Do you accept book acknowledgments? The Bible is silent on that.) When I think about everything that has ever meant anything to me, all roads lead back to you. You are the one clear thing that makes sense in a world gone mad. You have always felt safe to me, even when your church and some of your people didn't. Thank you for entrusting me with this message. Thank you for setting me free and for being entirely, eternally trustworthy. I know you are good. I know you love us. I know you're with us. I know you're for us. That's enough for me for the rest of this life. I love you so much.

NOTES

Chapter 1

1. Brené Brown, *Braving the Wilderness* (New York: Random House, 2017), 40–41.
2. Dallas Willard, *Renovation of the Heart* (Colorado Springs: Navpress, 2012), 199.
3. "Type Three," The Enneagram Institute, https://www.enneagraminstitute.com/type-3.

Chapter 2

1. Jessica Bennett, "Why We Need to Stop Calling Powerful Women 'Bitches,'" Cosmopolitan.com, March 8, 2014, https://www.cosmopolitan.com/career/advice/a5890/powerful-women-names/.
2. Kimberly Key, "The Fear Behind Women in Power," psychologytoday.com, August 19, 2016, https://www.psychologytoday.com/us/blog/counseling-keys/201608/the-fear-behind-women-in-power.
3. Shannan Martin, *The Ministry of Ordinary Places* (Nashville: Thomas Nelson, 2018), 21–22.

Chapter 3

1. "Body Image and Nutrition: Fast Facts," Teen Health and the Media, https://depts.washington.edu/thmedia/view.cgi?section=bodyimage&page=fastfacts.

2. "Body Image & Eating Disorders," National Eating Disorders Association, https://www.nationaleatingdisorders.org/body -image-eating-disorders.

3. Vanessa Van Edwards, "Body Types Through History," *Science of People*, https://www.scienceofpeople.com/ideal-body-types -throughout-history/.

4. Tina Fey, *Bossypants* (New York: Little, Brown and Co, 2011).

5. Jacqueline Howard, "The History of the 'Ideal' Woman and Where That Has Left Us," CNN.com, last modified March 9, 2018, https:// www.cnn.com/2018/03/07/health/body-image-history-of-beauty -explainer-intl/index.html.

6. "Statistics & Research on Eating Disorders," National Eating Disorders Association, https://www.nationaleatingdisorders.org /statistics-research-eating-disorders.

7. Hillary L. McBride, *Mothers, Daughters, and Body Image* (New York: Post Hill Press, 2017), 99.

8. McBride, 98–99.

9. McBride, 130.

10. Neva Piran, "*Journeys of Embodiment at the Intersection of Body and Culture Book Interview*," interview, Eating Disorders Resource Catalogue, May 31, 2018, https://www.edcatalogue.com /journeys-embodiment-intersection-body-culture-book- interview/.

11. McBride, *Mothers, Daughters, and Body Image*, 98.

12. McBride, 110.

13. Elizabeth Gilbert (@elizabeth_gilbert_writer), "You guys, I can't do it anymore. I can't attack myself. . .," Instagram post, December 28, 2018, https://www.instagram.com/p/Br9BmwRHMLN/.

Chapter 4

1. Darlene Lancer, "How to Know If You're a Victim of Gaslighting," psychologytoday.com, January 13, 2018, https://www .psychologytoday.com/us/blog/toxic-relationships/201801 /how-know-if-youre-victim-gaslighting.

2. Dr. Kristin Neff, "Why Women Need Fierce Self-Compassion,"

Self-Compassion, https://self-compassion.org/women-fierce-self
-compassion/.

3. Suzanne Lachmann, "How to Finally Feel Good Enough to Deserve
   Better," psychologytoday.com, Oct. 03, 2013, https://www
   .psychologytoday.com/us/blog/me-we/201310/how-finally-feel
   -good-enough-deserve-better.

4. Mark Leary, et al., "Self-Compassion and Reactions to Unpleasant
   Self-Relevant Events: The Implications of Treating Oneself Kindly,"
   Journal of Personality and Social Psychology 92, no. 5 (May 2007):
   889–904, https://doi.org/.

5. Anne Lamott, *Bird by Bird: Some Instructions on Writing and Life*
   (New York: Pantheon Books, 1994).

Chapter 5

1. Lisa Ferentz, "Why Asking for Help Is Hard to Do," psychologytoday
   .com, April 5, 2017, https://www.psychologytoday.com/us/blog
   /healing-trauma-s-wounds/201704/why-asking-help-is-hard-do.

2. Louis Laves-Webb, "Why Asking for Help Can Be a Challenging
   But Necessary Skill Set," Louis Laves-Webb, LCSW, LPC-S &
   Associates, August 3, 2017, https://www.louislaves-webb.com
   /why-asking-for-help-can-be-challenging-but-necessary/.

3. Teresa Amabile, Colin M. Fisher, and Julianna Pillemer, "IDEO's
   Culture of Helping," *Harvard Business Review*, from the January–
   February 2014 Issue, https://hbr.org/2014/01/ideos-culture
   -of-helping.

4. Wayne Baker, "5 Ways to Get Better at Asking for Help," *Harvard
   Business Review*, December 18, 2014, https://hbr.org/2014/12
   /5-ways-to-get-better-at-asking-for-help.

5. [NEED INFO]]

Chapter 6

1. "Theory," Center for Self-Determination Theory, http://
   selfdeterminationtheory.org/theory/.

2. Brooke Feeney and Nancy Collins, "A New Look at Social Support:
   A Theoretical Perspective on Thriving Through Relationships,"

Society for Personality and Social Psychology, August 14, 2014, https://doi.org/10.1177/1088868314544222.

3. Quora contributor, "Loneliness Might Be a Bigger Health Risk than Smoking or Obesity," Forbes, Jan 18, 2017, https://www.forbes.com/sites/quora/2017/01/18/loneliness-might-be-a-bigger-health-risk-than-smoking-or-obesity/#221f3acc25d1.

4. Brené Brown, *Braving the Wilderness* (New York: Random House, 2017), 52–53.

5. Maria Popover, *Figuring* (New York: Pantheon, 2019), 151.

6. Beth Berry, "In the Absence of 'the Village,' Mothers Struggle Most," *Motherly*, https://www.mother.ly/life/in-the-absence-of-the-village-mothers-struggle-most.

7. Thomas Farragher, "When a Newton Family Welcomed a Baby Who Is Deaf, 20 Neighbors Learned Sign Language," bostonglobe.com, February 7, 2019, https://www.bostonglobe.commetro/2019/02/07/farragher/TEREscjAx7jPNA7RP1IQoI/story.html?p1=AMP_Recirculation_Pos7.

8. Berry, "Absence of 'the Village.'"

9. Jen Hatmaker, *For the Love: Fighting for Grace in a World of Impossible Standards* (Nashville: Thomas Nelson, 2015), 117–118.

Chapter 7

1. Kate Torgovnick May, "Shonda Rhimes' message at TED2016: Say 'yes' to what scares you, even if it's saying 'no' to work," *TED Blog*, February 15, 2016, https://blog.ted.com/shonda-rhimes-tells-her-story-at-ted2016/.

2. Sara Robinson, "How to Positively Nurture Your Child's Competitive Spirit," afineparent.com, January 2017, https://afineparent.com/positive-parenting-faq/competitive-spirit.html.

3. Robinson, "Competitive Spirit."

4. Sumitha Bhandarkar, "What Every (Great) Parent Should Know About the Mindset of Success," afineparent.com, March 2014, https://afineparent.com/mindset/growth-mindset-introduction.html.

Chapter 8

1. "3 Reasons You Should Say YES More Often," Power of Positivity, September 3, 2014, https://www.powerofpositivity.com /3-reasons-say-yes-often/.
2. Kathryn J. Lively, "Why Women Have a Hard Time Saying No," psychologytoday.com, November 2, 2013, https://www .psychologytoday.com/us/blog/smart-relationships/201311 /why-women-have-hard-time-saying-no.
3. Cheryl Strayed and Steve Almond, "The Power of No, Part 2: Oprah Winfrey," July 22, 2017, in *Dear Sugars*, produced by Alexandra Leigh Young, podcast, MP3 audio, 25:09. https://www.wbur.org /dearsugar/2017/07/22/dear-sugars-oprah-two.
4. Greg McKeown, *Essentialism* (New York: Crown Business, 2014), 22.
5. Torgovnick May, "Shonda Rhimes."
6. McKeown, 137–139.

Chapter 9

1. Sarah Bessey, *Out of Sorts: Making Peace with an Evolving Faith* (Brentwood, TN: Howard Books, 2015), 88.
2. "Healthy and Unhealthy Religion," *The Evangelical Liberal*, November 5, 2011, https://evangelicaliberal.wordpress.com/2011 /11/05/healthy-and-unhealthy-religion/.
3. Tom Roberts, "The Inevitable, Necessary Crisis," *National Catholic Reporter*, May 13, 2009, https://www.ncronline.org/news/parish /inevitable-necessary-crisis.
4. Pete Enns, "The Bible, Wisdom, and Our Sacred Responsibility," peteenns.com, https://peteenns.com/the-bible-wisdom-and-our -sacred-responsibility/.
5. Rachel Held Evans, *Inspired: Slaying Giants, Walking on Water, and Loving the Bible Again* (Nashville, Thomas Nelson, 2018), 23–24.

Chapter 10

1. *Merriam-Webster*, s.v. "advocate (v.)," https://www.merriam-webster .com/dictionary/advocate.

2. Dacher Keltner, "The Compassionate Instinct," *Greater Good Magazine*, March 1, 2004, https://greatergood.berkeley.edu/article /item/the_compassionate_instinct.

Chapter 11

1. http://www.theliarinyourlife.com/conversation.php.
2. Susan Steen, "Secrets Eat Away Good and Leave Destruction Behind," *Daily News Journal*, last modified November 7, 2015, https://www.dnj.com/story/life/2015/11/06/secrets-eat-away -good-and-leave-destruction-behind/75289808/.
3. Dr. Blanton, *Radical Honesty: How to Transform Your Life by Telling the Truth* (Sparrowhawk Press, 2005).
4. Brittany Wong, "Radical Honesty 'Scares The Hell Out of People,' But It Could Be Worth Trying," huffpost.com, last modified February 18, 2019, https://www.huffpost.com/entry/radical -honesty-relationships_n_5baa7b26e4b0f143d10e0f88.
5. Dr. Jane Nelson, "Family Meetings," Positive Discipline, https:// www.positivediscipline.com/articles/family-meetings.
6. Carol Kinsey Goman, "Is Your Communication Style Dictated by Your Gender?" Forbes, March 31, 2016, https://www.forbes.com /sites/carolkinseygoman/2016/03/31/is-your-communication -style-dictated-by-your-gender/#3894a45deb9d.
7. Vinita Mohindra and Samina Azhar, "Gender Communication: A Comparative Analysis of Communicational Approaches of Men and Women at Workplaces," *Journal of Humanities and Social Science* 2, no. 1, (Sep-Oct. 2012), 18-27, http://iosrjournals.org/iosr-jhss /papers/Vol2-issue1/D0211827.pdf?id=5636.
8. Ariane Hegewisch and Emma Williams-Baron, "The Gender Wage Gap by Occupation 2017 and by Race and Ethnicity," Institute for Women's Policy Research, April 9, 2018, https://iwpr.org /publications/gender-wage-gap-occupation-2017-race-ethnicity/.
9. "Employment, Education & Economic Change: Pay Equity & Discrimination," Institute for Women's Policy Research, https:// iwpr.org/issue/employment-education-economic-change/pay -equity-discrimination/.

10. "Quotable Quote," Alice Walker, Goodreads, https://www
.goodreads.com/quotes/15083-the-most-common-way-people-give
-up-their-power-is.

Chapter 12

1. Dr. Henry Cloud and Dr. John Townsend, *Safe People* (Grand Rapids: Zondervan, 1995), 38–39, 168.

2. Victor E. Frankl, *"Man's Search for Meaning* Quotes," https://www
.goodreads.com/work/quotes/3389674-trotzdem-ja-zum-leben
-sagen-ein-psychologe-erlebt-das-konzentrationslag

3. Cloud and Townsend, *Boundaries* (Grand Rapids: Zondervan, 1992, 2017), 87.

4. Cloud and Townsend, *Boundaries*, 102–103.

5. Cloud and Townsend, *Safe People*, 180–181.

6. "Quotable Quote," C. S. Lewis, Goodreads, https://www.goodreads
.com/quotes/9123226-you-can-t-go-back-and-change-the
-beginning-but-you.

Chapter 13

1. Kent Eilers, "Henri Nouwen on Writing," *Theology Forums*, March 18, 2013, https://theologyforum.wordpress.com/2013/03/18
/henri-nouwen-on-writing/.

ABOUT THE AUTHOR

J en Hatmaker is the author of the *New York Times* bestseller *Of Mess and Moxie* (plus twelve others) and happy hostess of a tightly knit online community where she reaches millions of people each week. She hosts the wildly popular For the Love Podcast which was a Webby Award Finalist and won the People's Choice Podcast Award. She gathers thousands of women around a love of reading in the Jen Hatmaker Book Club. She and her husband, Brandon, founded the Legacy Collective, a giving community that grants millions of dollars to fund sustainable solutions to systemic issues around the world. They also starred in the popular series *My Big Family Renovation* on HGTV and stayed married through a six-month remodel. Jen is a mom to five, a sought-after speaker, and a delighted resident of Austin, Texas, where she and her family are helping keep Austin weird. For more information, visit jenhatmaker.com.

Enjoy Jen's Other Books

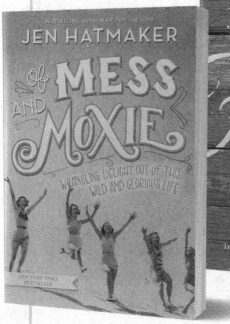

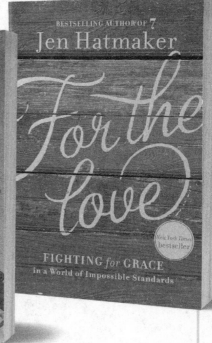

the ultimate
chat session
with Jen!

FOR THE LOVE of
people, home, stories, shoes, fitness,
family, friends, Jesus, faith,
community, TV, accessories, food,
culture, and so much more!

Listen In!

JENHATMAKER.COM/PODCAST

Jen Hatmaker
BOOK CLUB

Discover new chapters. Read with friends.
Connect with Jen. Have so much fun.

JENHATMAKERBOOKCLUB.COM

Join the Club!